The Rational Guide To

Extending SSIS 2005
with Script

PUBLISHED BY

Rational Press - An imprint of the Mann Publishing Group
710 Main Street, 6th Floor
PO Box 580
Rollinsford, NH 03869, USA
www.rationalpress.com
www.mannpublishing.com
+1 (603) 601-0325

ISBN-10: 1-932577-25-4
ISBN-13: 978-1-932577-25-9
Library of Congress Control Number (LCCN): 2007921557
Printed and bound in the United States of America.
10 9 8 7 6 5 4 3 2

Trademarks

Mann Publishing, Mann Publishing Group, Agility Press, Rational Press, Inc.Press, NetImpress, Farmhouse Press, BookMann Press, The Rational Guide To, Rational Guides, ExecuGuide, AdminExpert, From the Source, the Mann Publishing Group logo, the Agility Press logo, the Rational Press logo, the Inc.Press logo, Timely Business Books, Rational Guides for a Fast-Paced World, and Custom Corporate Publications are all trademarks or registered trademarks of Mann Publishing Incorporated.

All brand names, product names, and technologies presented in this book are trademarks or registered trademarks of their respective holders.

Disclaimer of Warranty

While the publisher and author(s) have taken care to ensure accuracy of the contents of this book, they make no representation or warranties with respect to the accuracy or completeness of the contents of this book and specifically disclaim any implied warranties or merchantability or fitness for a specific purpose. The advice, strategies, or steps contained herein may not be suitable for your situation. You should consult with a professional where appropriate before utilizing the advice, strategies, or steps contained herein. Neither the publisher nor author(s) shall be liable for any loss of profit or any other commercial damages, including but not limited to special, incidental, consequential, or other damages.

Credits

Author:	Donald Farmer
Technical Editor:	Ashvini Sharma
Editorial Director:	Jeff Edman
Book Layout:	Molly Barnaby, Kim Turner
Indexer:	Christine Frank
Series Concept:	Anthony T. Mann
Cover Concept:	Marcelo Paiva

All Mann Publishing Group books may be purchased at bulk discounts.

The Rational Guide To

Extending SSIS 2005
with Script

Donald Farmer
Group Program Manager
SQL Server Integration Services
Microsoft Corporation

**RATIONAL
PRESS**

An imprint of the **mann**™
PUBLISHING GROUP
www.mannpublishing.com

About the Author

Donald Farmer is the Group Program Manager of the SQL Server Integration Services team at Microsoft. Donald has worked with SQL Server Business Intelligence tools since they first made an appearance in SQL Server 7.0, first working in Scotland for an independent software vendor before joining Microsoft itself. A well-known speaker at SQL Server events, Donald frequently draws on experiences from his varied career—which includes construction, archaeology, and fish farming—to illustrate the importance of analytic software in the real world.

Acknowledgements

Naturally, this book would not have been conceivable without the work of the SQL Server Integration Services team. They are a remarkable bunch—painstaking, imaginative and talented. They well deserve the success and recognition I am sure they will achieve. Sergei Ivanov's persistent and inventive work on the scripting features of SSIS deserves special mention for this book.

Ashvini Sharma has been a tireless colleague and a good friend. His comments have helped to improve this book immeasurably, but any errors are mine.

Kamal Hathi and Bill Baker have supported me continuously with endless opportunities to develop and deepen my understanding of the technical and practical aspects of Business Intelligence.

Tony Mann and Jeff Edman have been equally tireless for Mann Publishing—their considerable patience is matched by their commitment and proficiency.

Alison and Matthew—without them nothing would be possible.

Dedication

For rtalison and itssounfair

About Rational Guides

Rational Guides, from Rational Press, provide a no-nonsense approach to publishing based on both a practicality and price that make them rational. Rational Guides are compact books of fewer than 224 pages. Each Rational Guide is constructed with the highest quality writing and production materials—at an affordable price. All Rational Guides are intended to be as complete as possible within the 224-page size constraint. Furthermore, all Rational Guides come with bonus materials, such as additional chapters, applications, code, utilities, or other resources. To download these materials, just register your book at www.rationalpress.com. See the instruction page at the end of this book to find out how to register your book.

Who Should Read This Book

This books is written for new users of SQL Server Integration Services who need to quickly implement additional functionality. Scripting is not just for developers—in fact, this book's approach aims to provide IT Professionals specifically with tools to enhance their processes. Nevertheless, code developers should find much of interest here too. The book is not a beginner's guide to all the features of SSIS. It assumes some basic knowledge of building and executing packages, even if just from working through the tutorials and samples that ship with the product. However, the book's systematic approach should help even new users to work through all the examples to build practical and useful scripts.

Conventions Used In This Book

The following conventions are used throughout this book:

▶ *Italics* — First introduction of a term.

▶ **Bold** — Exact name of an item or object that appears on the computer screen, such as menus, buttons, dropdown lists, or links.

▶ `Mono-spaced text` — Used to show a Web URL address, computer language code, or expressions as you must exactly type them.

▶ **Menu1⇨Menu2** — Hierarchical Windows menus in the order you must select them.

Tech Tip:
This box gives you additional technical advice about the option, procedure, or step being explained in the chapter.

Note:
This box gives you additional information to keep in mind as you read.

FREE *Bonus:*
This box lists additional free materials or content available on the Web after you register your book at `www.rationalpress.com`.

⚠ *Caution*
This box alerts you to special considerations or additional advice.

Contents

Contents

Contents

Introduction

Chapter 1

An Overview of SQL Server Integration Services

Information technology is an ever more pervasive factor in business. However, as the use of technology grows, so do certain common problems. In particular, there is a challenge in making sense of all the data that a business manages and stores. This issue can be crushing for large and small enterprises alike. The operational database may be quite different from, and mismatched with, the customer-management system. Spreadsheets used for budgeting may need data from legacy accounting applications. However, those applications may not export their data in a way that users can easily control.

Business Intelligence is an approach to solving many of these issues. It especially aims to give enterprises "one version of the truth." At one time, Business Intelligence (BI), was for large enterprises only. However, today even a small company may handle complex data in large volumes from e-business. Escalating regulation also requires corporations to have greater awareness of all their systems and data.

In this atmosphere, creating a unified view of the diverse data in a business is very demanding. *Data Integration* is a rapidly growing sector that attempts to overcome the obstacles raised by the diversity of data—obstacles that stand between you and that elusive "one version of the truth."

What is SQL Server Integration Services?

SQL Server Integration Services (SSIS) is a new data integration application in the SQL Server 2005 Business Intelligence suite. It is easy to understand the place of SSIS in this suite when you consider how Microsoft sums up their BI offering: "Integrate, Analyze, and Report."

Figure 1.1: SQL Server Business Intelligence Value Chain.

To this end, Microsoft SQL Server includes three BI applications:

▶ **Integration Services** — Brings together data from varied sources in a high-performance data integration platform.

▶ **Analysis Services** — Enhances integrated data with business rules and semantics, with caching for better performance.

▶ **Reporting Services** — Provides the presentation layer for delivering integrated and analyzed data to end users.

Moreover, these are not just stand-alone products. Each integrates well with others in the suite, and all feature well-supported APIs. The result is that SSIS is a true platform for data integration. In the same way, Analysis Services and Reporting Services are platforms to enhance the BI value chain.

> *Note:*
>
> In earlier versions of SQL Server, there was a simpler integration tool: Data Transformation Services (DTS). DTS was popular and easy to use, but it was limited in its power. Its architecture was also rather difficult to develop further. The SQL Server BI team therefore designed and developed SSIS as a new application from the ground up. SSIS is a successor to DTS, rather than a new version of that application.

Data Integration

Developers and analysts alike are in danger of over-using the word *integration* when discussing enterprise software. We regularly talk of *Enterprise Application Integration* (EAI) and *Enterprise Information Integration* (EII.) We can add to this *Customer Data Integration* (CDI) and various other acronyms such as ETL, MDM, and ELT. As the industry joke has it, this all begins to sounds like Old MacDonald's Farm. All that is missing is EIEIO!

All these technologies have a common aim: to enable users to work across multiple applications that were not designed to co-operate. Sometimes, this can be as simple as a single dashboard presenting reports from distinct sources. In a more advanced form, this scenario may use federated queries or EII.

In other cases, IT departments must enable the business logic of applications to work together. Typically, this includes an EAI tool such as Microsoft's BizTalk Server. However, the business logic layer is often cumbersome. Sometimes the volume of data is too great to use business logic efficiently. In other cases, applications are isolated in the IT environment. In such cases, the practical solution may be to integrate applications through their data.

The most widely seen result of data integration is the *data warehouse*. This is a high performance schema, optimized for reporting and analysis. Businesses use data warehouses to provide that "one version of the truth" for many users. To populate this central authoritative store, the administrator or architect must perform numerous data operations. They must extract data from their various source systems. They will transform this data to match the warehouse schema. Most likely, they will also clean the data to meet operational standards. Finally, the data will be loaded into the warehouse tables. This process—*Extraction, Transformation, and Loading (ETL)* —is a mainstay of data integration. SSIS is, first, an excellent ETL tool. It has features expressly designed to make the design and maintenance of data warehouses more productive and reliable.

The transformational aspect of ETL distinguishes it from other data integration technologies. ETL tools must handle large data volumes and run as scheduled jobs. Many administrators see replication and bulk data transfer as data integration too. However, *transformation* enables a broader spectrum of uses. Indeed, more and more we see data integration beyond the data warehouse. A good example is the management of master or reference data. Data syndication to and from internal or external sources can also leverage common ETL strengths.

With SSIS, you can drive these scenarios, and more. SSIS features event handling, support for Web services and the ability to connect any ADO.NET application to an SSIS data flow. With SSIS, you can mine data for patterns and exceptions during the integration process. All these features enable solutions that are more dynamic and adaptive than traditional integration. SSIS moves beyond ETL into an exciting new field.

Tools and Utilities

To build and manage these scenarios, SSIS provides an inclusive toolset:

▶ **Business Intelligence Development Studio** — This is the version of Visual Studio that ships with SQL Server 2005. BI developers use the studio to design, debug, and deploy their solutions. You can use Integration Services, Analysis Services, and Reporting Services all together in this environment. The studio hosts the SSIS *Designer*. This includes drag-and-drop design, visual debugging, and flexible deployment. Users with Visual Studio installed too, can manage code and Web projects in the same solutions as BI projects. In this way, you can combine source control and version control for projects that were quite separate before.

▶ **SQL Server Management Studio** — This is a shared environment for system administrators. You can now manage BI applications together, along with SQL Server itself and Notification Services. In particular, for SSIS, you can manage storage, security, and monitoring across many machines.

▶ **The SQL Server Agent Subsystem** — Scheduled jobs are essential to most ETL scenarios. *SQL Server Agent* is a scheduling system within SQL Server. The SSIS subsystem ensures that SSIS can take advantage of Agent features. For example, you can execute an SSIS process on a remote server using the T-SQL stored procedure sp_start_job.

▶ **dtexec and the Package Execution Utility** — Although scheduled jobs are an ETL priority, there will be times when you just need to run a package once. A command-line utility for these cases is dtexec. It has several switches to define a specific execution. The switches for dtexec are so complete that SSIS also includes a Package Execution Utility. This provides a user interface to build the command line syntax easily.

▶ **dtutil** — This is also a command line utility. You can use this for moving packages between stores, or for encrypting or signing them.

▶ **SQL Server Import-Export Wizard** — In previous versions of SQL Server, this wizard was a DTS feature. It was often the first (sometimes the only) experience users had of that application. This was apt, as DTS was rather simple. You could easily drive its features from a wizard-based user interface. In SQL Server 2005, SSIS underlies the Import-Export Wizard. Nevertheless, it is best to think of it as a SQL Server utility rather than as an entry point to SSIS. Why is this? Because the features of SSIS are diverse and powerful, while the wizard can only create the simplest packages. The wizard is excellent for moving data quickly and easily between systems. However, most BI users will need the more complete features of SSIS. For these users, it is good advice to begin with the BI Development Studio.

Note:

Beneath the user interface of SSIS, you will notice that the object model and command line tools (such as dtexec and dtutil) still have names reminiscent of DTS. This is simply because the working title of SSIS was still DTS until quite late in the product cycle! Microsoft renamed the application to reflect its new architecture and features. However, renaming every object and interface would have disrupted beta customers and partners. Do not let this application "archaeology" mislead you. SSIS is an entirely new application. Perhaps it is best to see the object names as a warm acknowledgement of a popular predecessor!

Editions

SSIS is available in SQL Server 2005 Workgroup, Standard, and Enterprise Editions:

▶ **Workgroup Edition** — This new edition of SQL Server includes the SQL Server Import-Export Wizard. Workgroup Edition includes only this wizard for data integration. The BI Development Studio is not available.

▶ **Standard Edition** — This includes the BI Development Studio and therefore the SSIS Designer. Note that there is no throttling of performance in this edition. Standard edition offers the full power of SSIS together with the greater part of its features.

▶ **Enterprise Edition** — This complete edition includes everything in Standard edition. However, it also has some advanced and original features. In this edition, SSIS includes data cleansing with fuzzy logic, text mining, and for the Data Flow, Analysis Services and Data Mining support.

Why Use SQL Server Integration Services?

It may appear flippant to turn this question around and ask instead, "Why not?" Nevertheless, customers are perhaps more likely to turn the question on its head. Easy, high performance, extensible data integration is now on hand at no extra cost with SQL Server. This is itself one of the most popular and fastest-growing enterprise database systems. Why look elsewhere?

Not only is SSIS available with the database, it has its own benefits to consider for data integration solutions:

▶ **Developer productivity** — SSIS uses the BI Development Studio for drag-and-drop development. It includes visual debugging and an effective build-and-validate model for impact analysis.

▶ **BI integration** — Analysis Services, Data Mining, and Reporting Services can all share objects and metadata with SSIS. This enables the rapid development of complete, end-to-end BI solutions.

► **Management integration** — In a diverse enterprise, SQL Server Management Studio brings great benefits. It delivers capable administration of relational and OLAP databases, reporting, and data integration across many servers in a single environment.

► **Performance** — Data Integration can be challenging in the volume of data and complexity of its processes. SSIS shows first-rate performance on commodity, mainstream, and high-end systems.

► **Community and partner ecosystem** — These are not features as such, but they *are* a great benefit for developers and managers alike. The huge international community of SQL Server users ensures that SSIS skills and training will be widely available. It also ensures that users will share and discuss best practices vigorously and openly. Indeed, the SSIS technical forum on MSDN is one of the most active of all Microsoft online communities (see `https://forums.microsoft.com/msdn/showforum.aspx?forumid=80`). Similarly, the far-reaching SQL Server partner program encourages many independent companies and developers to extend the SSIS feature set. This will add features such as geo-spatial data handling, special data quality processes, and connectivity to legacy or other specialized systems.

FREE *Bonus:*

Great performance is one of the key advantages of SSIS. However, getting the best performance also requires great measurement tools to give that extra insight. What could be better than tools that you define yourself? If you register this book at `www.rationalpress.com`, you can download bonus Chapter A. This includes details of how to script your own performance monitors to measure SSIS in action.

However, you may sometimes find that SSIS, or even the partner program, does not offer some functions that you require. For such cases, scripting is powerful and practical. Scripting in SSIS enables you to add new, fully integrated, functions easily. With this in mind, we hope that this short book will prove a valuable companion in helping you achieve your enterprise data integration needs.

Summary

SQL Server Integration Services is a significant application in Microsoft's Business Intelligence offering. Its aim is to enable enterprises to meet their technical and business demands for deeper analysis, in a world of ever more diverse data in greater volumes.

Although SSIS includes many compelling features out-of-the-box, it is above all an extensible platform for building solutions. Scripting is the easiest way to leverage that platform, by extending SSIS with customized features.

Chapter 2

SQL Server Integration Services Architecture

As you might expect, an application like SSIS has several components. It is valuable to understand these components and their uses when developing and managing integration solutions. This chapter introduces the SSIS architecture. Rather than examining the object model in the abstract, we shall start with the features that drive the key use cases of SSIS. From there, we will work our way out to a broad architectural overview. The purpose is not to be a detailed and technical architecture reference, or a beginner's tutorial. Rather, this chapter will give the user a good grasp of the SSIS elements that will power their designs and applications.

Basic Elements

Let's start by reviewing the basic SSIS elements.

Data Flow

The primary use case of SSIS is to move data. In the simplest scenario, a user extracts data from a source and loads it to a destination. However, except when doing a basic import or export of data, things are rarely so straightforward. Users may need to consolidate data from several diverse sources. That may require a number of transformation processes. Even the targets may be diverse.

The architecture of the SSIS data flow engine addresses these data movement and transformation needs. It is a true data pipeline. That is to say, it enables data to flow from one or many sources in one process, through multiple transformation steps, before directing the data to one or many destinations. As a pipeline, this engine is capable of parallel execution and it handles the memory demands and threading models needed for performance and reliability.

The data flow is discussed in the section "More About Data Flow," later in this chapter. For now, we can visualize it quite simply. In Figure 2.1, you can see it as a many-source, many-operation, and many-destination pipeline.

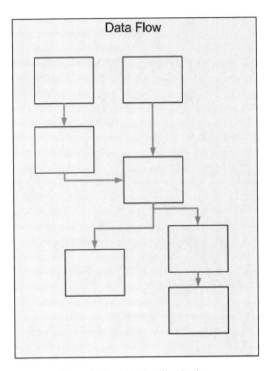

Figure 2.1: Schematic View of the Data Flow Pipeline.

> # *Note:*
>
> In whitepapers, presentations, and webcasts about SSIS, you will often read or hear references to "the pipeline." This is simply another name for the Data Flow Task and the high-performance data-handling architecture it contains.

Tasks

In SSIS terms, this pipeline process is a *task*—the *Data Flow Task*. That is to say, it is a single "unit of work." When executed at runtime, it either succeeds or fails, or perhaps just completes or is cancelled.

SSIS includes many additional tasks. This is because there are often other "units of work" that need to be executed to complete your integration process, although the Data Flow Task is by far the most important feature in SSIS.

For example, it may be necessary to truncate a table before loading it with new data. You could do that using an *Execute SQL Task* before the Data Flow Task. Similarly, once the data is loaded, we may want to send an e-mail to the administrator to confirm that the data is now ready for use. You can do this with a *Send Mail Task*. Figure 2.2 shows these tasks.

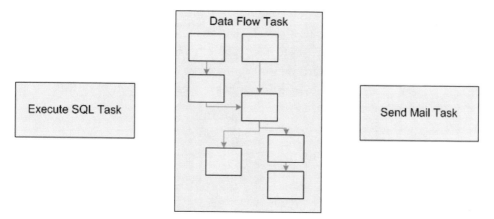

Figure 2.2: Schematic View of Some SSIS Tasks.

SSIS includes many such tasks. For example, there are tasks for Web service or Microsoft Message Queue integration; tasks for working with Windows Management Instrumentation; and tasks for working with files in the file system, or with XML documents. Of course, one of the most interesting tasks, and a core subject of this book, is the *Script Task*, which enables you to add your own units of work to SSIS.

Precedence Constraints

In the previous section, we outlined a simple but realistic scenario. We truncated a table with an Execute SQL Task, loaded it with data using a Data Flow Task, and then sent an e-mail with a Send Mail Task. These three tasks are, in this case, dependent on each other. Loading new data before truncating the table would lead to the loss of the new data.

Sending an e-mail before the data load completes could be misleading. Moreover, you only want to send a notification of success if the data load really was successful. If the data load failed, perhaps due to a table lock, you may need to perform a different action. At the least, you may feel like sending a very different email!

In SSIS, the developer creates these logical chains of tasks with *precedence constraints*. A precedence constraint between two tasks ensures that the second task only executes if certain conditions are true after the first task has finished. Typically, the condition is simply the result (success, failure, or completion) of the previous task. Without precedence constraints, all our tasks would generally execute in parallel.

More advanced uses of constraints are also possible. For example, you can evaluate complex expressions using variables to meet precise conditions before executing another task. Figure 2.3 shows a simplified view of our three tasks, now chained with precedence constraints, and a fourth task—to send a disgruntled e-mail if the Data Flow Task should fail to load our table!

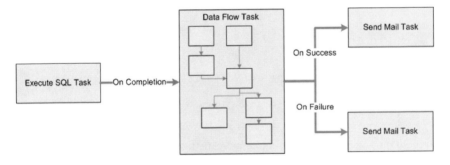

Figure 2.3: Schematic View of SSIS Tasks and Precedence Constraints.

Control Flow and Containers

Taken together, tasks and precedence constraints comprise *Control Flow*—the basic workflow of an integration process. Your Control Flow can have just one task if you like, or it may have many tasks of many types. In complex scenarios with many tasks, you may need to group functionally related tasks together. Alternatively, you may wish to loop over a related set of tasks repeatedly—for example, to handle a number of different source files in a similar manner. SSIS includes container objects for these needs, in particular a *Sequence* container, a *ForEach Loop* and a *For Loop*.

Figure 2.4 shows our familiar scenario, with a sequence added. If the Data Flow Task succeeds, we still want to send an e-mail to the admin, but now we also want to process an Analysis Services cube. However, processing the cube and sending the e-mail can, and should, happen in parallel. To do this, we have grouped them in a sequence and constrained the sequence to execute if the Data Flow Task succeeds. Within the sequence, the mail and cube processing tasks execute in parallel.

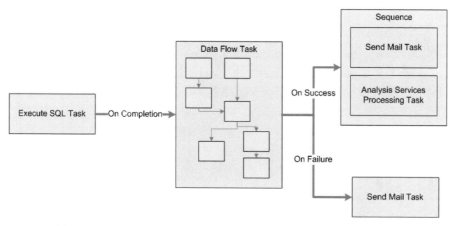

Figure 2.4: Schematic View of SSIS Tasks, Precedence Constraints, and Containers.

The SSIS Package

Wrapping all these objects is a special container—the SSIS package. Having designed your data integration with data flows and tasks and containers, you will wish to execute it and perform all the operations you have designed. A package is the object that contains the full definition of your Control Flow, with all its tasks and other objects. When you save your work, you save a package—it is an XML document. When you deploy your work, you deploy a package.

> **Note:**
>
> If you are familiar with Object-Oriented Design, you will likely have already guessed that containers are basic objects in the SSIS model. A package is a special container, which in turn can contain other containers such as sequences or loops. In fact, a container called the Task Host wraps, or hosts, every task in SSIS, although you will rarely be aware of this unless you are developing custom tasks.

Variables and Property Expressions

In almost any software development scenario, variables are an essential feature for holding values so that different objects can use them. In SSIS, a package can contain variables for use by tasks and other objects. Moreover, we shall see that they are particularly useful when writing scripts. In the scenario we have been describing, a variable could hold the name of the OLAP cube for processing, or the name of the person to whom we will send the notification email.

An SSIS task, for example, can use the value stored in a variable using a *property expression*. In this way, any task property that you can edit can be dynamically set at runtime. Some tasks also have special properties that can reference variables.

Tech Tip:

SSIS features a powerful expression language based on a C syntax. Package developers can use this language in several ways. For example, an expression can calculate new column values in a data flow. You can also use an expression to evaluate conditions on a precedence constraint. Property expressions enable SSIS developers to change the value of a property at runtime with the full power of the expression language. The developer references variables with the symbol @ (the asperand or commercial at). For example, the To property of our Send Mail task can take its value from a variable called *ToName* with an expression such as:

```
@ToName + "@myenterprise.com"
```

Variables in SSIS are *scoped* to containers. That is to say, variables are only visible inside the container in which the developer creates them. For example, a package contains all other containers, so a variable created in a package is visible to all other containers in that package. However, a variable created in a sequence container is only visible to the sequence container and tasks within the sequence. A variable created in a task is only visible to that task.

Variables in general can contain values of many types, but individual variables have a specific DataType, such as **String**, **DateTime**, or **Int32**. This restricts the data that developers can store in a single variable.

SSIS also includes many *system variables* that hold values reflecting the current package and its execution, such as ExecutionStartTime, UserName, MachineName, and a unique ExecutionInstanceGUID.

Chapter 5 includes more information on variables, in particular how to create them for use in your scripts.

Connection Managers

As you might expect for a data integration application, the ability to connect to data stores is fundamental to SQL Server Integration Services. *Connection managers* are objects that provide important connection services for tasks and other objects in a package.

When a package is running, the connection managers, as their name perhaps suggests, manage the physical connectivity to the databases or other data sources and destinations. At design time, connection managers enable the SSIS developer to define connection strings for these connections, and to validate the connection string and other properties.

SSIS provides many standard connection managers, for connectivity to common data stores such as Text Files, ADO.NET, OLEDB, Analysis Services, and even SQL Server Mobile Edition. Developers will typically use these connections to data stores in the data flow. SSIS also includes connection managers for technologies such as WMI, MSMQ, SMTP, and FTP, which developers will more often use in the Control Flow.

The SSIS Developer creates a connection manager in a package, where many objects can use it, but unlike variables, connection managers do not have scope. When two or more objects use the same connection manager, they will typically share a runtime connection. However, it is possible to create two separate connection managers, each pointing to the same database. In such a case, your two connection managers will create two separate physical connections.

Chapter 9 includes more information on connection managers, including how to reference them in your scripts.

Events

There is another type of container to consider in SSIS: *event handlers*. You can think of event handlers as a special kind of sequence container. Event handlers contain other containers and tasks. However, rather than executing when a constraint is true (or in parallel with other tasks when the package starts) an event handler executes when an event occurs. For example, you can create an event handler that will execute if an error occurs on a specific task, or in the package.

In the scenario we have been building up, we currently execute a Send Mail Task if the Data Flow Task fails, using a precedence constraint. We could use an event handler instead, which will execute on the **OnError** event of the Data Flow Task. Alternatively, you could add an event handler for OnError event of the package itself, therefore sending your indignant e-mail if *any* error occurs during execution. Data flow is still the heart of data integration, but you can see that SSIS provides a wealth of further functionality to handle this core functionality capably and dependably.

You will learn more about events in Chapter 5, especially how to use them in your scripts.

The Runtime Engine and Configurations

Now that we have reviewed the architecture of an Integration Services package, we can consider what happens when the package executes.

The SSIS runtime engine handles all the features we have described thus far—tasks, connection managers, variables, precedence constraints, and so on. This engine also provides support for transactions, logging, and checkpoint restart for failed packages.

One important runtime feature of Integration Services is the use of *configurations*. A configuration stores certain property or variable values separately from your package. The runtime engine applies those values when the package executes.

For example, you could save the value of a connection string in an XML file as a configuration. The runtime engine reads the value from the XML file and applies it to the package. In this way, an administrator could provide different XML files for different connection strings on different servers, without ever having to edit the package itself. Configurations, therefore, make it easy to move packages from development to test to production. Each environment may need a different connection string that you can store in a different configuration.

Caution:

Configuration of connection strings is a very common scenario. Nevertheless, for security, SSIS will remove any clear-text passwords when saving or configuring packages. The best and most secure way of making connections is to use Windows Authentication. In this case, the password is not required anyway. However, if you cannot benefit from Windows Authentication, you may use the Protection Level property of an SSIS package. This enables you to encrypt sensitive data, such as connection strings, or even the entire package. You should always try to avoid situations where you find yourself placing a password in a configuration. If you can really find no alternative, given your security infrastructure, then you should ensure that the configuration stores the password in a Windows Registry key, a database table, or in a file, with stringent security permissions.

There are several kinds of supported configurations including XML files, the Microsoft Windows Registry, a SQL Server database table, or environment variables. You can provide multiple configurations for a package. With some forethought, you can even share configurations between packages. We will see configurations in action in Chapter 5, when we will use them with a Script Task to set important properties at runtime.

The SSIS Designer

As an Integration Services user, you will quickly become familiar with the Business Intelligence Design Studio in general and the SSIS Designer in particular. We will not introduce a full tutorial for new users here, as that is beyond our current scope. However, this book will show you numerous Designer techniques, useful for beginners and practiced users alike.

Figure 2.5 shows the SSIS Designer with an empty SSIS package already open. This is the default view you will see when you create a new SSIS project. The Designer creates an empty package for each new project and opens it by default.

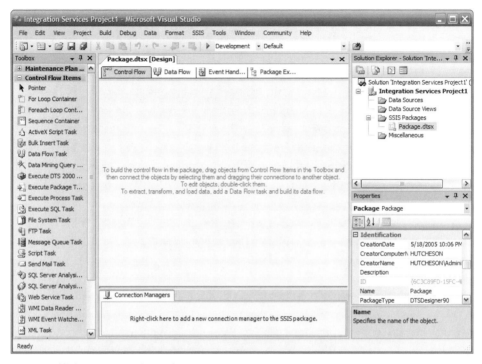

Figure 2.5: SQL Server Integration Services Designer.

On the right-hand side of the screen is the **Solution Explorer**, where projects are created and managed. An SSIS project includes a **Packages** folder, and it is here that you can add and remove packages from your project.

Also shown on the right-hand side is the **Properties** window. When you select an SSIS object in the Designer, you can view and edit some its generic properties here. Be aware, however, that you must edit some properties (perhaps with complex dependencies), with special editors for the selected object.

As you can see in Figure 2.5, the SSIS Designer has four tabs. The four tabs are for **Control Flow**, **Data Flow**, and **Event Handlers**, and one final tab for exploring a package in a tree view.

As described earlier, data flow is actually a task, but a very special one. In fact, data flow has its own Designer tab to enable you to build complex flows visually. However, even though you can have many Data Flow Tasks in a package, there is only one Designer tab for data flow. You select which specific Data Flow Task to view by double-clicking your selected task in the Control Flow designer. The view will switch to the **Data Flow** tab with your selected Data Flow Task open. Alternatively, you can switch between individual tasks in this view using the combo box shown in Figure 2.6.

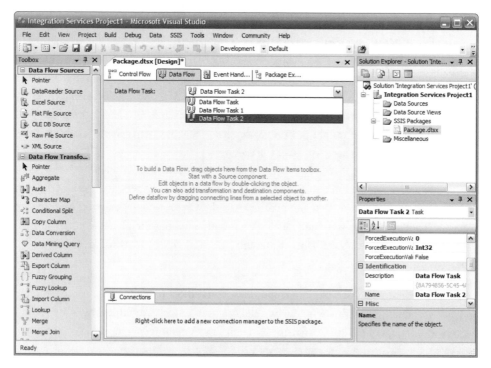

Figure 2.6: Selecting a Data Flow Task in the Data Flow Tab.

When you execute a package in the Designer, it reveals another tab, to show progress including execution messages. Once the package has finished, you can still view the details shown on the **Progress** tab. It remains open, but is now labeled **Execution Results**, and shows the progress of the prior execution.

Note:

There are various ways to execute a package in the Designer. The simplest is to open the package you wish to execute and press F5. Alternatively, you could select Debug⇨ Start Debugging from the Designer menu. However, if you have more than one project in your solution (for example, an Analysis Services project), these methods may give unexpected results. They may deploy the Analysis Services project! This is because in a Visual Studio solution with multiple projects, one project will be the startup project. You start this project with the F5 key, or with the Start Debugging command. You can set a new startup project using the right-click contextual menu of the project in the Solution Explorer. Another way to execute a package is to right-click the package itself in the Solution Explorer. Select Execute Package. Only the selected package will execute.

You add and edit connection managers in the **Connection Managers** area seen at the foot of the screen in Figure 2.6. You can add tasks to the Control Flow designer by dragging from the **Toolbox** on the left-hand side or by double-clicking the object in the **Toolbox**. When you are working in the **Data Flow** tab, you add components to your flow in the same way.

One useful window, not visible by default, is the **Variables** window. Here you can create and edit variables. Show this window by selecting the **SSIS⇨ Variables** menu item from the top-level menu of the studio. Figure 2.7 shows the **Variables** window.

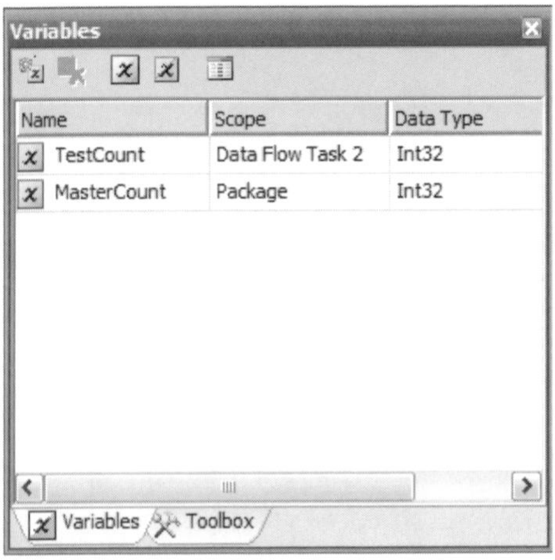

Variables
Name
Scope
Data Type
TestCount
Data Flow Task 2
Int32
MasterCount
Package
Int32
Variables
Toolbox

Figure 2.7: Variables Window.

You can add a variable by clicking the **Add Variable** button. Note that when you create a variable, you create it with the scope of the currently selected object. For example, if you had selected a Script Task and then created a variable, you could only use that variable in the Script Task. To create a variable with the scope of the package, first click on the background of the Control Flow designer. The **Variables** window also shows this variable scope. If you have variables of different scope, they will appear and disappear in the **Variables** window as you select different tasks and containers in the package.

System variables are typically read-only and not visible by default, but you can show them by clicking the grey **Show system variables** button in the **Variables** window.

SSIS Clients and the Service

The SSIS Designer that we have discussed is a special SSIS *runtime client*. That is to say, it connects to the SSIS runtime engine and requests services from it, such as package validation, enumeration of variables, and so on. When you run a package in the Designer, it uses another specialized client called the *debug host* for debugging. You will learn more about debugging SSIS packages in Chapters 4 and 7.

Other SSIS clients include the dtexec and dtutil utilities discussed in Chapter 1.

Bonus:

If you register this book at www.rationalpress.com, you can download the bonus Chapter B. This discusses the use of a very special client that enables Reporting Services or any ADO. NET application to leverage SSIS for integration scenarios.

The SSIS Service

This is a Windows service, which you use to manage packages in production. Unlike other features of the SSIS, you do not use the service in the BI Development Studio, but in the SQL Server Management Studio.

The SSIS Service enables you to:

▶ Monitor running packages, even on a remote machine, and request them to stop

► Import and export packages between the file system and SQL Server for storage

► Customize your storage folder hierarchy

Although SQL Server Setup installs the SSIS service, you must enable it manually the first time you wish to use it. After that, you can set it to start automatically if you wish. You can start or stop the service using the Services MMC snap-in or the SQL Server Configuration Manager, which you can see in Figure 2.8.

SQL Server Configuration Manager			
File **Action** **View** **Help**			
SQL Server Configuration Mana	Name	State	Start Mode
SQL Server 2005 Services	SQL Server Integration Services	Running	Automatic
SQL Server 2005 Network Co	SQL Server FullText Search (MSSQLSERVER)	Stopped	Automatic
SQL Native Client Configura	SQL Server (MSSQLSERVER)	Running	Automatic
	SQL Server Analysis Services (MSSQLSERVER)	Running	Automatic
	SQL Server Reporting Services (MSSQLSERVE...	Running	Automatic
	SQL Server Browser	Stopped	Other (Boot, Syste...
	SQL Server Agent (MSSQLSERVER)	Running	Automatic

Figure 2.8: SQL Server Configuration Manager Showing SSIS Services.

It is important to note that the SSIS service does not *execute* packages. It only monitors them. Even when you ask the service to stop a package, the service only requests the package to stop. In other words, the service is passive: it is a service and not a server. This means that if the service is disabled, you may still execute packages. However, you will not be able to monitor them or manage their storage.

The full range of features for SSIS package management, including security and deployment, are beyond the range of this book. However, there is excellent documentation for these features, and you can read detailed whitepapers on MSDN, and at http://www.microsoft.com/sql/bi.

More About Data Flow

As mentioned earlier in this chapter, the primary use case of SSIS is to move data. This, of course, means that the Data Flow Task is central to your work with SSIS. This section contains more details about the data flow and its components. This will be useful later on when we look at the script component, which enables you to extend the Data Flow Task with your own functions.

A data flow can include three types of components: sources, transformations, and destinations. Let's look at each:

► **Source components** — These have outputs, but do not have inputs. The data flow uses sources to extract data from an external source, often from text files or from database tables. However, sources are very versatile. They can source data from XML documents and other technologies too. You can also write your own sources using script, as you shall see in Chapter 9.

► **Transformation components** — These have both inputs and outputs. Transformation components generally modify the extracted data in some way. For example, a transformation may convert a column from a string type to a date type, or calculate the difference between two values in a row. A transformation may also shape the data, perhaps by aggregating it, or merging and joining data from two different inputs to a single output. Transformations are versatile, and you can write your own transform logic using scripts. See Chapters 7 and 8 for more details.

► **Destination components** — As you may expect, these have inputs but no regular outputs. Destinations typically deliver data to an external destination, such as a database table, or to other data stores such as text files. However, destinations have several other uses. A destination can simply be an ADO recordset in memory, or you could use a data destination to train an Analysis Services Data Mining model. You can also write destination components with scripts as you shall see in Chapter 9.

Because you can use scripts for sources, transformations and destinations, you could write an entire data flow using only script components!

Transformations

There is a wide range of pre-built transformation components available for you in SSIS. Some of the most common are:

► **Data Conversion** — Converts columns from one data type to another.

► **Derived Column** — Calculates a new column value based on an expression.

► **Merge** — Merges two inputs to a single output.

► **Sort** — Sorts the data by columns.

► **Aggregate** — Calculates aggregations, such as **Group By**, **Sum**, **Count**, and **Average**.

These components fall into two categories: *synchronous* and *asynchronous* components.

A synchronous component reads rows at its input, modifies these rows in some way, and delivers the rows at its output. The modifications may add new columns with new values, or may filter out rows. However, a synchronous component does not add new rows to the data flow. Even when adding new column values, such as a calculated value, a synchronous component will add them to an existing row that arrived at the input. We say that the output is *synchronous to the input*.

Because a synchronous component only transforms data within a single row, you might also think of them as *row transformations*. Good examples of these synchronous components are **Data Conversion** and **Derived Column**. Figure 2.9 shows data before and after a row transformation.

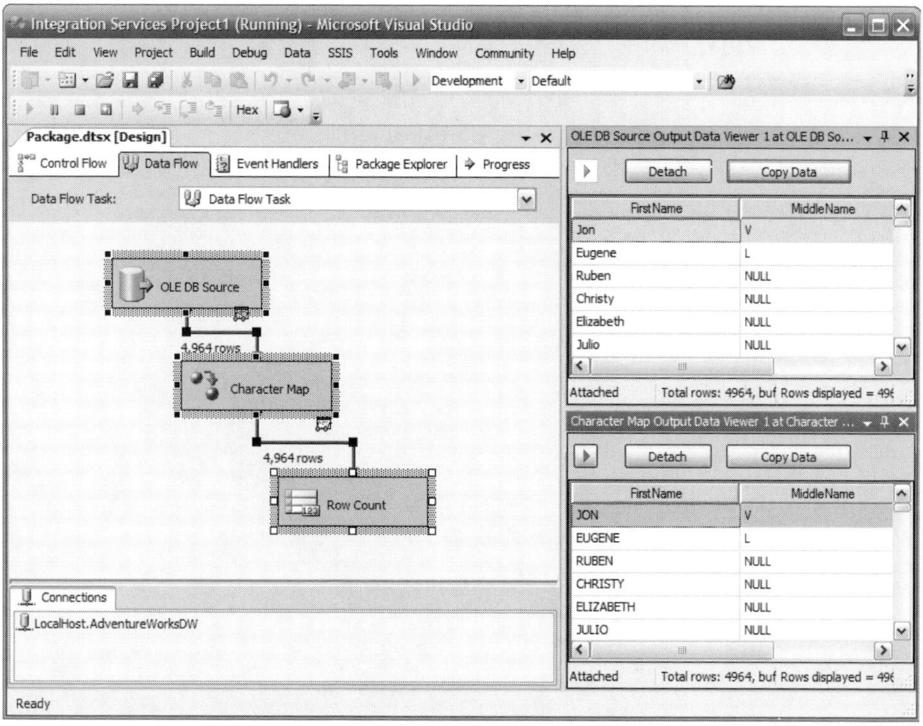

Figure 2.9: Row Transformation Component.

In contrast, an asynchronous component reads rows at its input, and delivers new rows at its output. The modifications may include joining rows from two different inputs into a new row, or calculating a completely new row based on incoming data. An asynchronous component always adds new columns at its output. We say that the output is *asynchronous to the input*.

Let's look at two sub-types of asynchronous component.

The **Merge** component joins rows from two inputs. As it finds incoming rows that it can merge, based on a sort key, it delivers these rows to the output. The output rowset is different from the incoming rowset, but the component works on each row individually. You can think of this type of asynchronous component as a rowset transformation, as opposed to the synchronous row transformation. Figure 2.10 shows data before and after a rowset transformation. Another common example is the **Union All** component, which can also join multiple rowsets.

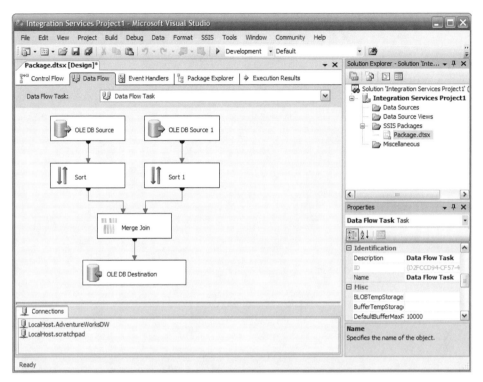

Figure 2.10: Rowset Transformation Component.

However, the **Aggregate** component is also asynchronous but behaves somewhat differently. If the aggregate is to calculate the average, maximum, or minimum value of a column (or even just a count), it must read every incoming row before it can complete its calculation. Moreover, in this case, the output rowset will have a very different shape from the incoming rowset. The **Aggregate** can count the number of distinct values in a string column, but the output value will be an integer. You can think of this type of asynchronous component as a *full rowset* transformation. It must see all the rows before completing its work. Sort is another example of this component type. Figure 2.11 shows data before and after a rowset transformation. Some SSIS users refer to these full rowset components as *blocking* transformations, because they effectively block the progress of the data through the data flow pipeline until they have seen every row.

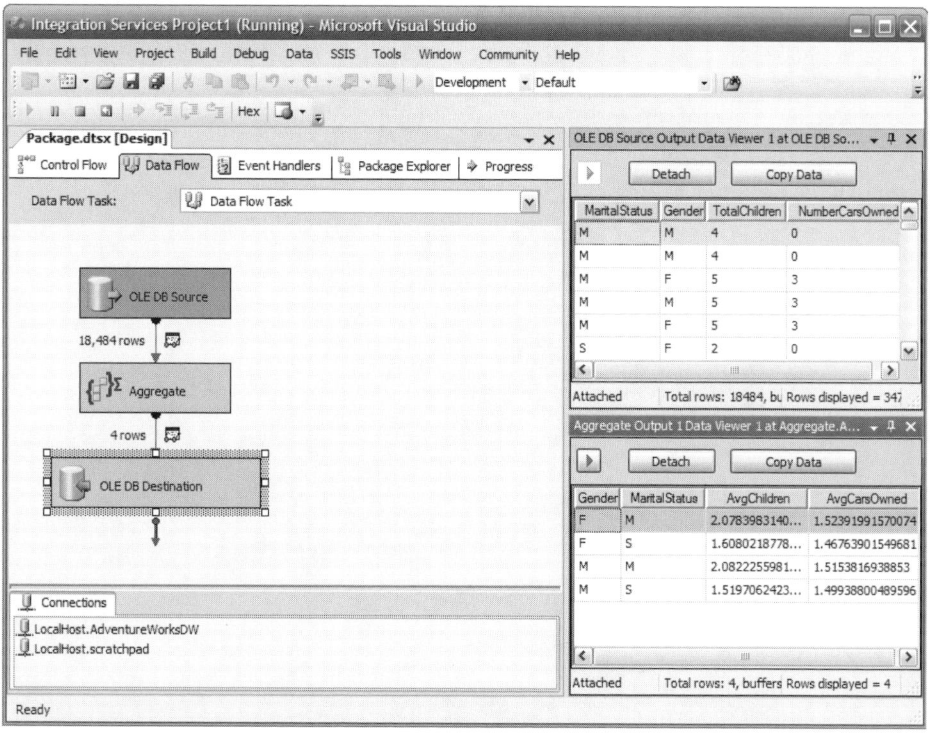

Figure 2.11: Full Rowset Transformation Component.

Tech Tip:

As you shall see later, a **Source** is a special kind of asynchronous component. It creates new output rows, but has no input rows at all. Similarly, a **Destination** is a special kind of synchronous component. It creates no new rows. Except for special cases of error handling, it delivers none of its incoming rows to an output.

Paths

When you connect the output of one component to the input of another, you create a *path*. Paths appear to be quite simple. However, they have some appealing properties and are very useful in the Designer.

For example, you can name a path and select to show that name on the Designer surface. This can be a useful annotation for complex packages. In fact, to make understanding a package easier, the SSIS Designer will automatically show the path name if there are several exclusive outputs from one component.

You access the name of a path by double-clicking it to view the **Path Editor** shown in Figure 2.12. This editor also enables you to see the metadata at any point in the data flow, including the columns at that point, and their data types.

Figure 2.12: Path Editor.

In addition, you can use the **Path Editor** to add *data viewers*. These enable you to debug your data flow visually with grids and data charts. You will learn more about data viewers in Chapter 7.

Summary

There are several components in the SSIS architecture. Knowing how these components work together will help you to build better applications. When you are extending SSIS with scripts, a working knowledge of the architecture will help there too.

Now that we have introduced SQL Server Integration Services and its architecture, it is time to explore the potential of scripting in this exciting application.

Chapter 3

SQL Server Integration Services Scripting

A *script* is computer code that you embed in your SSIS package.

A pre-built SSIS task, such as the Send Mail Task, is a separate object or library that a developer compiled. (The tasks that ship with SSIS were compiled at Microsoft.) You can install this task on your computer and use it in many SSIS packages. However, you only reference the compiled binary library, not the code that the developer used to build it. When you move your package (when deploying it to a server, for example) the code for the Send Mail task does not move with it. The Send Mail task must on the server for the package to run.

The code for a script, on the other hand, is stored inside your package and is part of it. Typically, you will write this code yourself. Only the package that contains the script can make use of that code. If you want to reuse the script, you must somehow copy it to another package.

Why Use Script?

SSIS includes a wide range of tasks and components for building Control Flow and Data Flow processes. However, even SSIS cannot cover every scenario that users will want to implement. In some cases, you may need to use a single function to transform data that SSIS does not provide. In other cases, you may have some existing code that you would like to use in SSIS.

With the open APIs of SSIS, developers can write custom tasks and components in any .NET language, such as C# or J#. To do this, they require an edition of Visual Studio that supports their programming language. Moreover, although SSIS is relatively easy to extend with custom code, developers still need good coding skills and disciplines to deliver effective extensions.

Scripting in SSIS is for users who wish to add new functions, but who do not wish to develop completely new components in Visual Studio or other .NET development environments. For example, BI developers, rather than code developers, or database administrators, will typically use scripting to extend SSIS when they need to. See Chapter 11 for details of why you might wish to create custom components.

The scripting capabilities of SSIS are relatively easy to use, compared to coding from scratch. However, do not make the mistake of thinking that it is simplistic or limited. It is possible to develop and debug very sophisticated operations with scripting. For example, a script task or component can reference external . NET assemblies quite easily. You can easily leverage powerful libraries such as the . NET Framework Cryptography or Math namespaces.

This power is not difficult to use. SSIS uses the Visual Studio for Applications (VSA) environment for developing scripts, so users have an integrated development environment (IDE) with features such as color-coded syntax highlighting and IntelliSense. Script Tasks can even be debugged line-by-line in this environment.

Some Scripting Considerations

There are two important ways to use script in SSIS—a *Script Task* for extending the Control Flow, and a *Script Component* for extending the data flow. However, first, you should know about a third scripting method, although you will use it only very rarely.

The ActiveX Script Task

In SQL Server 2000, DTS users were familiar with the *ActiveX Script Task*. This task enabled you write scripts in various scripting languages including vbscript and jscript. This was the only form of scripting in DTS.

SSIS also includes an ActiveX Script Task, but it is only included for backwards compatibility when a user migrates a DTS package to SSIS. You should not write new scripts using the ActiveX Script Task. The new scripting features of SSIS are more flexible, easier to use, and give much better performance.

VSA Scripting

The scripting you will use to extend SSIS leverages the Visual Studio for Applications (VSA) environment. With this environment, you can write scripts in VisualBasic.NET. Note that other .NET languages such as J# or C# are not available. Nor can you install other .NET languages for use with VSA.

Nevertheless, Visual Basic .NET *is* a fully featured programming language in its own right. It is easy to use, and because scripts in SSIS can be pre-compiled, it gives excellent performance.

Of course, you may already have custom functions written in another language. On the other hand, you may need to integrate work with developers who prefer to work in C# or J#, or even Borland Delphi for .NET. In these cases, you can still use this existing work, by compiling into a .NET assembly. You can reference that assembly from within your Visual Basic .NET script, and call functions within that assembly quite easily.

Summary

Scripting is the most convenient way for you to extend SSIS with custom functions. The scripting environment in SSIS is productive and powerful. Script Tasks are the easiest way to get started with scripting in SSIS. Therefore, in the next section, we will write some Script Tasks and through them learn about the VSA environment and its features.

Did you know?

If you have Visual Source Safe with Visual Studio, you can check in and check out SSIS projects just like any other code. In fact, you can manage code for all your Business Intelligence needs. For example, you can ensure that SQL scripts to create your data warehouse tables are always synchronized with the SSIS packages to load them, together with the Analysis Services cubes and Reports that you will use.

Script Tasks

Chapter 4

Your First Script Task

In Chapter 2, you learned about SSIS tasks and how they can be chained together to create a complex control flow. SSIS includes many different pre-built tasks that will meet most control flow needs. However, now and then, you may need some function that SSIS does not have out of the box. Help is at hand in the form of the Script Task, which will enable you to add your own Control Flow features easily. This chapter shows you how to build and debug a simple Script Task. Later, we will add features such as variables and events.

A Scenario for Scripting

SSIS packages often run as scheduled jobs. In fact, in Chapter 1 we noted that this was a core requirement for ETL tools. One reason these processes must run on a schedule is that they often run unattended overnight. At these times, the SSIS developer can take advantage of off-peak processing to use resources that may not be fully available during peak business hours. However, even these off-peak resources vary. For example, capacity may be quite different on the weekends than during the week.

Typically, an SSIS developer would write different packages for different days. The administrator would schedule each package separately. There may be a lot of shared logic between these processes. In this example, we will use a Script Task to write a package that "knows" which day of the week it is. It can therefore run different sequences of tasks, depending on its schedule.

Your first script task, therefore, should do the following:

▶   Calculate the day of the week.

▶   If it is a weekday, return Success.

▶   If it is a weekend, return Failure.

In this way, you can constrain one sequence of tasks with an **OnSuccess** precedence constraint from this task. This sequence will only execute on weekdays. You can constrain another sequence with an **OnFailure** precedence constraint. This sequence will only execute at the weekend.

The Structure of a Script Task

When using script in a package, there are two "layers" to the Script Task to consider. There is the script itself (the code you will write to perform your operations) and an SSIS task that "wraps" the script and embeds it in the control flow of the package.

The properties of the task include the name and description, and options such as whether to pre-compile the script to binary code, and for handling variables. When developing a Script Task in your package, you will edit both the task properties and the script.

Adding a Script Task to Your Package

Your scheduling Script Task will be the first task in a package, because this task determines whether to execute a weekday or weekend sequence of tasks. You will therefore start with an empty SSIS package.

Note:

This chapter assumes you have at least some familiarity with building an SSIS package. You should at least be familiar with the simplest examples from the documentation or the samples that ship with the product.

Preparing the Package

Use these steps to prepare a package:

1. Create a new SSIS Package.

2. In the Designer, drag a **Script Task** from the **Control Flow Items** tab of the **Toolbox** to the **Control Flow** design surface. You can see the **Script Task** in the **Toolbox** in Figure 4.1.

    Ensure it is the **Script Task** you select and not the **ActiveX Script Task**. The **ActiveX Script Task** is only included with SSIS for legacy support of migrated DTS packages.

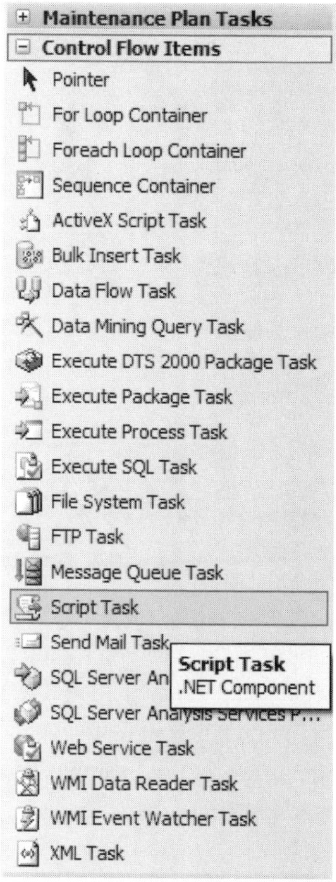

Figure 4.1: Control Flow Items Toolbox Showing the Script Task.

Editing the Script Task Properties

Follow these steps to edit the Script Task properties:

1. Double-click the **Script Task** shape on the designer surface to open the **Script Task Editor**. You can see the **Script Task Editor** in Figure 4.2.

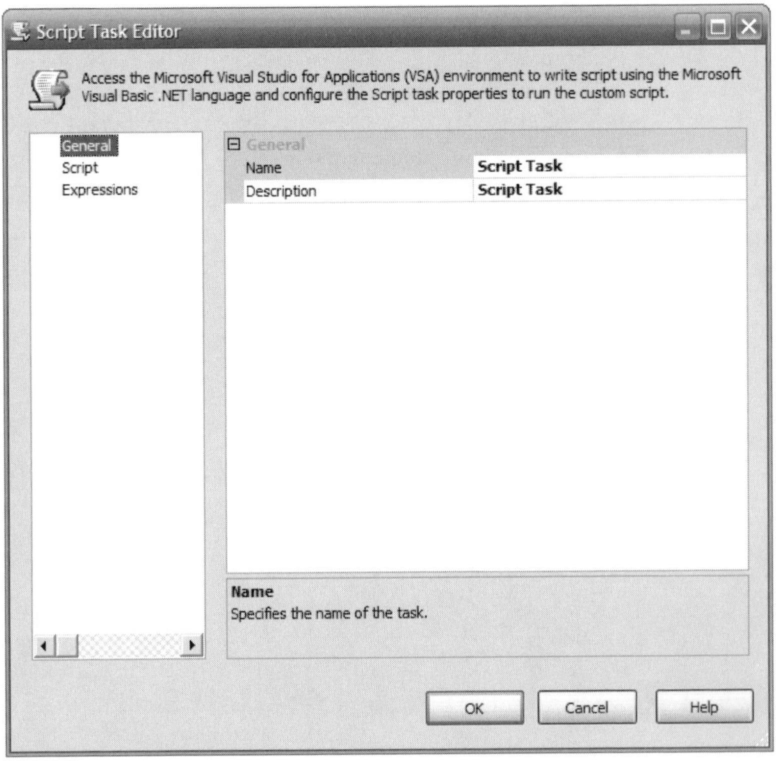

Figure 4.2: General Tab of the Script Task Editor.

2. The editor opens by default at the **General** tab. On this tab, you should give the task a suitable name and description. Make it a practice to give your tasks useful names and descriptions. You will find it helps greatly when you or someone else looks at your package in the future. In this example, name the task `Schedule script task` and enter a description such as `Script to determine weekend and weekday logic`.

3. Now select the **Script** tab, using the list view on the left of the **Script Task Editor**. Figure 4.3 shows the **Script** tab selected.

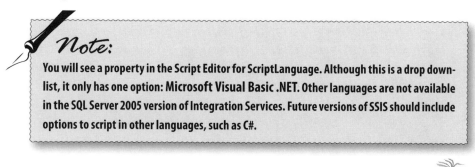

Figure 4.3: Script Tab of the Script Task Editor.

For our first Script Task, it is not strictly necessary to edit any of the properties on this page. We will discuss them in Chapter 5.

Note that the **Pre-compile** property is True by default—this ensures best performance of your script by compiling it to binary code in advance. If the property was False, SSIS would need to compile the script when the package runs, and this would affect performance. Nevertheless, remember that SSIS scripts are never interpreted, so the performance of the new scripting features in SSIS is generally much better than the scripting features of the older DTS product.

Note:

You will see a property in the Script Editor for ScriptLanguage. Although this is a drop-down list, it only has one option: Microsoft Visual Basic .NET. Other languages are not available in the SQL Server 2005 version of Integration Services. Future versions of SSIS should include options to script in other languages, such as C#.

Opening the Scripting Environment

The steps so far have involved editing the task properties—the "outer layer" discussed earlier. Now it is time to edit the script itself. On the **Script** tab of the **Script Task Editor**, click the **Design Script…** button at the bottom right (see Figure 4.3). Clicking this button opens a fully featured development environment for your script.

The VSA Environment

The environment in which you develop scripts is hosted in Visual Studio .NET. When you start this environment by clicking the **Design Script** button in the **Script Task Editor**, another Visual Studio window opens on your desktop. This title of this window is **Microsoft Visual Studio for Applications** and it contains a default project and script for you, as you can see in Figure 4.4. We generally call this environment VSA for short.

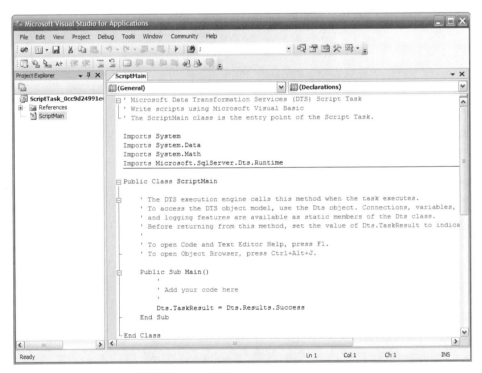

Figure 4.4: VSA environment with Default Project and Script.

As you can see in Figure 4.4, there are many menu options and toolbar choices in VSA. As it happens, several of these options are not relevant to scripts embedded within SSIS. For now, we will work through the features of this environment, as you require them for SSIS scripts.

The Default Script

In Figure 4.4, you can see the default script that SSIS provides when you first edit a Script Task. This script is fully functional. You can run a package containing a Script Task with only this script, but it will not do much! However, there are important features to this script that you should understand. Let us walk through it.

First, as shown in Listing 4.1, there are a few lines of comments, simply describing the task. You can certainly add your own comments here if you like. Simply prefix a line with a single quote to make it a comment.

```
' Microsoft SQL Server Integration Services (SSIS) Script Task
' Write scripts using Microsoft Visual Basic
' The ScriptMain class is the entry point of the Script Task.
```

Listing 4.1: Header Comments in the Default Script.

The Imports Statements

The next lines of the script are **Imports** statements. SSIS adds these to make it easier for you to call functions in other libraries. By default, some .NET Framework system libraries and the SSIS runtime are included here. The default **Imports** statements for an SSIS Script Task are shown in Listing 4.2.

```
Imports System
Imports System.Data
Imports System.Math
Imports Microsoft.SqlServer.Dts.Runtime
```

Listing 4.2: Default Imports Statements for a Script Task.

The ScriptMain Class

SSIS executes a script by calling a class at runtime. When SSIS creates a **Script Task**, the default class has the name **ScriptMain**.

It is possible for your script to include additional classes. If you preferred your new class to be the default, you would modify the **EntryPoint** property shown in Figure 4.3 to the name of your new class. However, for your first script, and for most scripts that you write, **ScriptMain** will be sufficient. SSIS provides the code shown in Listing 4.3 for the **ScriptMain** class.

```
Public Class ScriptMain

    ' The DTS execution engine calls this method when the task executes.
    ' To access the DTS object model, use the Dts object. Connections,
    ➲  variables, events,
    ' and logging features are available as static members of the Dts class.
    ' Before returning from this method, set the value of Dts.TaskResult to
    ➲  indicate success or failure.
    '
    ' To open Code and Text Editor Help, press F1.
    ' To open Object Browser, press Ctrl+Alt+J.

    Public Sub Main()
        '
        ' Add your code here
        '
        Dts.TaskResult = Dts.Results.Success
    End Sub
End Class
```

Listing 4.3: ScriptMain Class.

> ✎ *Note:*
>
> This book does not include a detailed tutorial on Visual Basic .NET, or a detailed introduction to Visual Studio .NET. A great deal of help is available through the online documentation for the application itself. For example, select the word Public in the default script and press the F1 key. Visual Studio .NET will show help for the Visual Basic .NET Class statement, including its modifiers. This level of help is available throughout the scripting environment.

Within the ScriptMain class (between `Public Class ScriptMain` and `End Class`) SSIS declares Main. This is the default subroutine of the class. The code for this subroutine is in Listing 4.4:

```
Public Sub Main()
    '
    ' Add your code here
    '
    Dts.TaskResult = Dts.Results.Success
End Sub
```

Listing 4.4: Main Subroutine.

This code includes comments, as usual, but also one significant line of code that sets the **TaskResult** to **Success**. You will remember from the brief overview of tasks in Chapter 2 that every task is a unit of work that either succeeds or fails. The **TaskResult** property determines this end state. **TaskResult** takes a value from the **Dts.Results** enumeration – it can be either **Success** or **Failure**.

> ⚠️ *Caution:*
>
> Your default script sets a **Success** return value explicitly. Without it, the task would *still* succeed, but this line ensures that the behavior of the task is clear to you. This is important. If the logic of your script means that a task must fail in some circumstances, then you *must* also explicitly set a **Failure** return value on that code path.

Note the **Dts** namespace. Chapter 1 includes a note on the history of SSIS, explaining why the namespace is still **Dts**!

Editing the Script

To edit your script you need do nothing more than type your code in place, between the comment `Add your code` here, and the code that sets the `TaskResult`. However, the Visual Studio .NET environment includes useful features such as IntelliSense for building scripts more easily.

To create your scheduling code, edit the ScriptMain subroutine as shown in Listing 4.5:

```
Public Sub Main()
    '
    ' Add your code here
    'Dim t As String
    t = Now.DayOfWeek.ToString
    If t = "Saturday" Or t = "Sunday" Then
        Dts.TaskResult = Dts.Results.Failure
    Else
        Dts.TaskResult = Dts.Results.Success
    End If
End Sub
```

Listing 4.5: Code to Determine if a Package is Running on the Weekend.

This listing is very simple, but it has some features worth noting. First, notice that the script explicitly casts DayOfWeek to a string. This is because Option Strict is On by default for these projects. You could change this by adding the line Option Strict Off at the start of the script before any Imports statements, but this is not good practice. The **Strict** option ensures that you will catch many errors at design time, not at runtime, and it improves performance.

Another feature of this simple script is that it includes code paths that explicitly lead to success or failure. To this end, the line Dts.TaskResult = Dts.Results.Success has been moved to within the **If** statement.

Did you also notice that, as you typed, IntelliSense provided a list of valid options for completing statements, as in Figure 4.5? This makes building a valid script much easier.

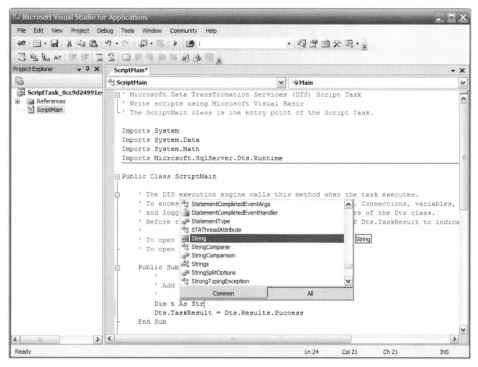

Figure 4.5: IntelliSense Suggests Options for Completing a Statement in the Script.

Running a Package with a Script Task

Follow these steps to run the script to see if it performs properly:

1. Close the script editor by choosing the **File⇨ Close and Return** menu item, or pressing **Alt+Q**. In fact, you may also close the window using the system menu. You do not have to save the script. VSA will do this for you.

2. Click the **OK** button in the **Script Task Editor** dialog box to return to the BI Development Studio.

3. Now you can run the package as usual by pressing **F5**, or choose the **Debug⇨ Start Debugging** menu item from the main menu. Another way to execute a package is to right-click the package itself in the **Solution Explorer**, and select **Execute Package**.

When you run the package, watch the behavior of the Script Task. It should turn red and report a failure in the designer if the package is running on a Saturday or Sunday. On the other hand, it should turn green and report success if the package is running on a weekday.

If you are working through these examples over the weekend, you should consider swapping the success and failure paths of this script. Set **Success** if the package is running at the weekend and **Failure** if the package runs on a weekday. In this way, if the task fails you will know it is the result of an error. This may save you some confusion when debugging your script

You could extend this package by adding tasks chained with an **OnSuccess** or **OnFailure** precedence constraint from this task.

Tech Tip:

When you close the VSA environment, the script is automatically saved. When you close the Script Task editor window, the script is automatically compiled to binary code if the pre-compile option is enabled. If you ever need to recompile the script—perhaps to move it from a 32-bit to a 64-bit environment, or between service packs of VSA that have slightly different binary formats—you can force a recompile by opening the script editor, making a minor change such as adding a space, and then closing the VSA environment and the Script Task Editor window.

Summary

Building a script task is easy. Drag the component from the toolbar, rename it, and open the VSA editor. Even developing the script is straightforward. Features like IntelliSense help you to write valid scripts rapidly.

Now you have built your first script task, and perhaps it is already quite useful for you. A simple script can immediately add some useful functionality to SSIS. In fact, once you are proficient with scripting, you will find that it may become the most useful feature in your toolbox. In the next chapter, we will add some additional functionality and you will learn how to debug the task in detail.

Chapter 5

Integrating the Script Task with Your Package

At this point, you have a Script Task that tests for the current day. It returns either **OnSuccess** or **OnFailure** to the package. The return values are the only "communication" between the task and the package. This chapter shows how to integrate your scripts more closely with the rest of your package. This includes how to use variables and events, and how to log your script's execution. In addition, you will learn to debug the script for errors, and to ensure that it executes accurately.

First, let us consider some more details of the scenario. Currently, the script evaluates Now() when it reaches that line of code. Based on this, it returns success or failure. However, this may not be quite the expected behavior with a long-running package. Some very large and complex data loads may run for a few hours. (A full data warehouse refresh for example.) In such a case, the package could start before midnight of one day and continue into the next day. The system administrator may regard the package as starting on a weekday, but the script would evaluate it as a weekend package, or the other way round. We can cover this scenario in our script by evaluating the *start time* of the package, rather than simply Now(). In addition, it may be useful to get the *DayOfWeek* value back from the script in order to use it in other tasks. We will create a *DayOfWeek* variable to hold this value.

Using Variables with the Script Task

You will extend the script task now to use two different types of variable: a read-only system variable and the read-write user variable that you will create.

Adding a Variable to Your Package

Before using a variable in a script task, you must ensure that the variables you will use exist in the package *before* opening the Script Task Editor. You cannot add new package variables in the Script Task Editor.

Use the following steps to add the *DayOfWeek* variable that you shall use in your script.

1. Click anywhere on the design surface of the **Control Flow** tab to ensure that you create variable in the scope of the package. It will then be available to any task to use. In Chapter 2, we described the importance of variable scope.

2. From the main menu, choose **SSIS⇨Variables**. The **Variables** window will appear.

3. In the **Variables** window, click the **Add Variable** icon. This adds a new variable that will appear in the Variables window.

4. Using the **Name** column of the **Variables** window, change the name of this new variable to DayOfWeek.

5. In the **DataType** column of the **Variables** window, change the data type of this new variable to String.

6. In the **Value** column of the **Variables** window, ensure that the default value of this new variable is an empty string.

Now you are ready to use this new variable in your script. You should also save your package. As in any programming environment, it is good practice to save your work regularly.

Adding a Reference to a Read-Only Variable

When you execute an SSIS package, the runtime engine stores the package start time in a system variable that tasks and components can use. You can reference this system variable in your script, too. You will not change the value of this variable in the script. In fact, you could not even if you wanted to, because this system variable is read-only. Therefore, in the following steps, you will reference the start time as a read-only variable.

1. Double-click the **Script Task** shape on the design surface to open the **Script Task Editor**.

2. The editor opens by default at the **General** tab. You should select the **Script** tab, using the list view on the left of the **Script Task Editor**.

3. The system variable you will use is **StartTime**. Therefore, enter `StartTime` as the value for the **ReadOnlyVariables** property. Figure 5.1 shows this step in the **Script Task Editor**. Note that variable names are case-sensitive.

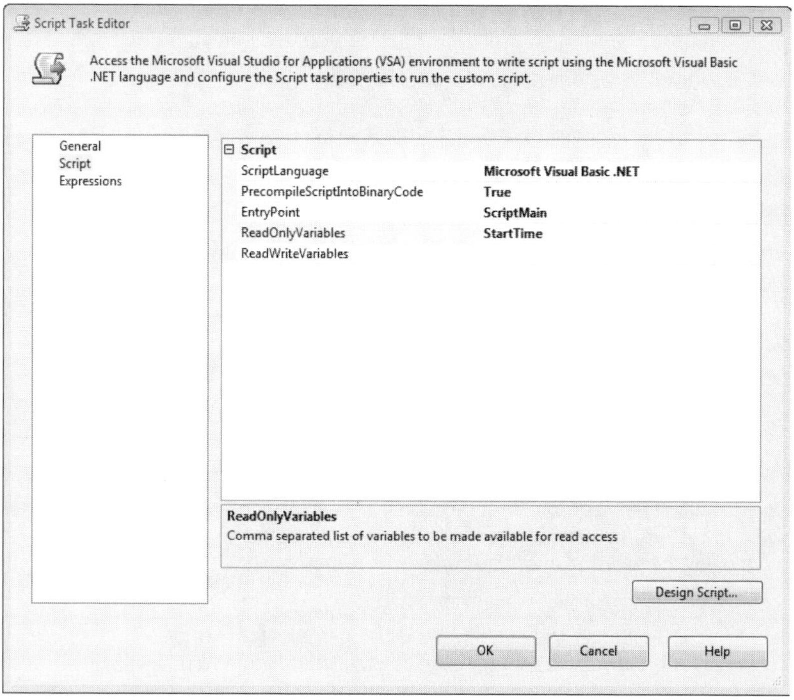

Figure 5.1: ReadOnlyVariables Property in the Script Task Editor.

In this case, you have referenced a system variable, which is read-only. However, you are not restricted to using system variables in this list. Any variable can be referenced here as a read-only variable. This list simply ensures that this instance of the Script Task cannot write to the listed variables. The list has no significance outside the scope of the Script Task that you are editing.

Points to Note When Adding a Reference to a Variable

You will often see system variables named with their fully qualified namespace, such as `System::StartTime`. You could use the fully qualified name here too if you like. However, because the variable name is unique in this case, this is not necessary.

The **ReadOnlyVariables** and **ReadWriteVariables** properties are comma-separated lists. If you need to refer to more than one variable in your script, remember to enter them all here, and separate the names with a comma. If you are entering only one variable name, as in our example, you do not need to add a comma.

Remember to add your variables to these properties in order to use them in a script. If you forget to do so, your script may still compile and not return a design-time error. However, when executing the package, the script will raise the error that you can see in Figure 5.2. This error tells you that the runtime engine could not be find the variable in the collection of variables used by the Script Task.

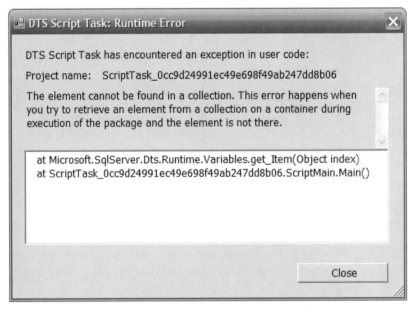

Figure 5.2: Error—A Variable is Not in the ReadOnlyVariables or ReadWriteVariables Properties.

Another common error is to forget that variable names are case-sensitive. Here too, the task will fail when executing.

Adding a Reference to a Read-Write Variable

Now you should add a reference to your user variable. Simply enter the name of the variable, DayOfWeek, as the value of the **ReadWriteVariables** property. Be sure to remember that the name is case-sensitive.

Using the Variable in Your Script

Listing 5.1 shows the sample script, modified to use the variables that we have just added.

```
Public Sub Main()
    '
    ' Add your code here
    '
    Dim t As String
    t = CDate(Dts.Variables("StartTime").Value).DayOfWeek.ToString
    Dts.Variables("DayOfWeek").Value = t
    If t = "Saturday" Or t = "Sunday" Then
        Dts.TaskResult = Dts.Results.Failure
    Else
        Dts.TaskResult = Dts.Results.Success
    End If
End Sub
```

Listing 5.1: Using a Variable in a Script.

This script calculates the day of the week from when the package started, rather than from when the script task executes. It also writes the name of the day of the week back to a user variable for use elsewhere in the package.

There are a number of points to note about this script:

▶ In the Script task, you always reference a variable as a member of the Dts. Variables collection. For example, you reference the *DayOfWeek* variable as Dts.Variables("DayOfWeek"). This reference is always case-sensitive.

▶ You always access the variable value for reading or writing via the **Value** property of the variable. For example, you read the value of the *StartTime* variable as Dts.Variables("StartTime").Value.

▶ Remember that Option Strict is On by default. The Value property of an SSIS variable is of Object type, in order to hold many types of variable values. Because of this you must explicitly cast Dts.Variables("StartTime").Value to a CDate in order to use it with the system DayOfWeek function. You must also explicitly use ToString to convert the result of the DayOfWeek function to a string. Option Strict only allows implicit data type conversions to *widening* conversions where data loss will not occur. So, when writing to the *DayOfWeek* variable, no explicit conversion is required.

Debugging the Script Task

There are two aspects to debugging your script task in SSIS: debugging the interaction of the script with your package and debugging the script itself.

Debugging the Task and Package

One great benefit of SSIS is its comprehensive debugging features. These reduce development times considerably, and enable you to find and fix problems easily, even in complex processes.

The most obvious feature for debugging is the color-coded progress reporting that you can see whenever you execute a package in the Designer. Color-coding informs you of the state of tasks in the Control Flow, and of components in the Data Flow. In the Control Flow, the following colors show you the state of tasks:

▶ **White** — The task has not yet started to execute.

▶ **Yellow** — The task is currently executing.

▶ **Green** — The task has succeeded.

▶ **Red** — The task has failed.

▶ **Grey** — The task is disabled.

As you have seen earlier in the discussion of errors, the Designer also shows a **Progress** pane. When debugging is finished, the Designer labels this the **Execution Results** pane, as shown in Figure 5.3. Note that you can select any message in this pane, right-click, and copy the message text to the clipboard.

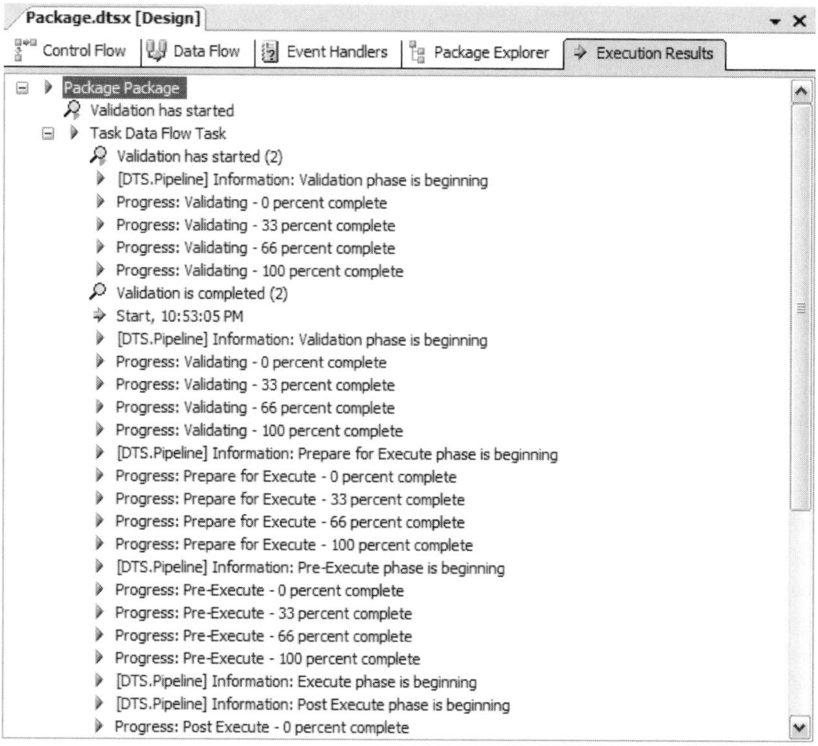

Figure 5.3: Execution Results Pane.

Messages that appear in the **Progress** pane also appear in the **Output** window. You can show this window by selecting **Debug⇨ Windows⇨ Output** from the Designer menu, or by the key combination **Ctrl+Alt+O**. This window is shown in Figure 5.4.

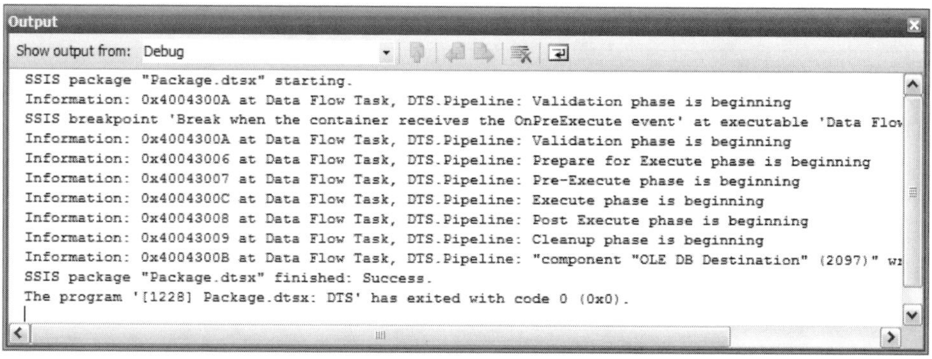

Figure 5.4: Output Window.

The **Output** window also shows some messages which do not appear in the **Progress** pane. In Figure 5.4, you can see that this includes messages about *breakpoints*. Breakpoints are one of the most useful debugging features in SSIS. A breakpoint pauses execution of a package, enabling you to examine properties such as variable values. You can then decide to continue with, or to cancel, execution of the package.

You can set breakpoints on any task (or container such as a loop or a sequence) with the following steps.

1. Right-click on the task or container, then select **Edit Breakpoints** from the contextual menu.

2. In the **Set Breakpoints** dialog box shown in Figure 5.5, select specific breakpoints that you wish to enable by clicking in the **Enabled** column for that row. A dark red dot should appear in the **Enabled** column.

3. A breakpoint usually pauses every time package execution reaches that point. However, you can modify this behavior by changing the **Hit count type** and **Hit count number** for any breakpoint you have enabled. In this way, you set the breakpoint to pause execution only when it has been hit a certain number of times. This is most useful for debugging loops.

It is also possible to set breakpoints on the package itself. To do this, right-click on the background of the Control Flow designer, and select **Edit Breakpoints** from the contextual menu.

Set Breakpoints - Data Flow Task   **? X**

Select the breakpoints in the task, For Loop, Foreach Loop, or Sequence to enable. Optionally, select the number of times a breakpoint is ignored before execution is suspended on the breakpoint.

Enabled	Break Condition	Hit Count Type	Hit Count
☑ ●	Break when the container receives the OnPreExecute event	Always	1
☐ ○	Break when the container receives the OnPostExecute event	Always	0
☐ ○	Break when the container receives the OnError event	Always	0
☐ ○	Break when the container receives the OnWarning event	Always	0
☐ ○	Break when the container receives the OnInformation event	Always	0
☐ ○	Break when the container receives the OnTaskFailed event	Always	0
☐ ○	Break when the container receives the OnProgress event	Always	0
☐ ○	Break when the container receives the OnQueryCancel ev...	Always	0
☐ ○	Break when the container receives the OnVariableValueCh...	Always	0
☐ ○	Break when the container receives the OnCustomEvent ev...	Always	0

[OK]   [Cancel]   [Help]

Figure 5.5: Set Breakpoints Dialog Box.

In Figure 5.5, you see that breakpoints are set on particular events. There are several of these, and tasks can have custom events. However, the ones you will use most commonly for breakpoints are:

▶ **When the task or container receives the OnPreExecute event** — Use this to examine the state of variables and other objects just before a package or control flow object executes. You can also set an OnPreExecute breakpoint by selecting an object and pressing **F9**.

▶ **When the task or container receives the OnPostExecute event** — Use this to examine the state of variables and other objects immediately after a package or control flow object executes. This is particularly useful when set on the package, because it enables you to examine the final state of all variables before finishing debugging.

▶ **When the task or container receives the OnError event** — This is, of course, useful for examining the state of objects in the event of an error.

► **When the task or container receives the OnTaskFailed event** — Use this to examine variables and objects if a task fails. Remember that a task failure need not be an error. In our script example, we cause the task to fail on purpose when executed on a weekend, in order to use success or failure to execute different sequences of tasks conditionally.

Other events are more advanced. You should consult the SSIS documentation for more information on these.

If you have set a breakpoint on a task, the breakpoint icon (a dark red dot) will appear in the task shape in the Designer. If you have set a breakpoint on the package, the breakpoint icon will appear on the **Control Flow** tab itself. You can see these breakpoint icons in Figure 5.6.

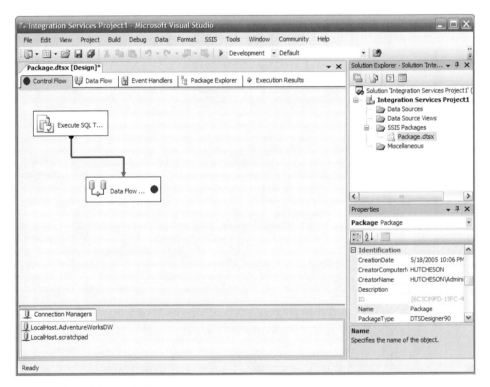

Figure 5.6: Breakpoint Icons in the Designer.

When you enable a breakpoint on an object, then execute the package, the package will execute as usual in the Designer until the breakpoint is hit. When the package hits a breakpoint and pauses, the Designer changes the breakpoint icon to a red dot containing a yellow arrow. This enables you to see the current breakpoint. Alternatively, you can show the **Breakpoints window** by selecting **Debug⇨Windows⇨Breakpoints** from the Designer menu or using **Ctrl+Alt+B**. The **Breakpoints** window shows you enabled breakpoints, and which one is currently pausing the package. Figure 5.7 shows the **Breakpoints** window during debugging, when the package has hit a breakpoint.

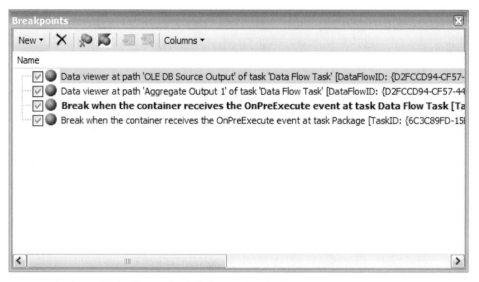

Figure 5.7: Breakpoints Window Showing that the Package Has Hit a Breakpoint.

To clear a breakpoint on a task or other object, simply right-click the object and select **Edit Breakpoints** from the contextual menu. You can now select which breakpoints you wish to clear. Alternatively, you could select the task or object and press **F9**—this clears *all* breakpoints on the object.

To debug your Script Task using breakpoints, follow these steps:

1. Right-click the **Script Task** in the **Control Flow** designer and select **Edit Breakpoints**.

2. Click in the **Enabled** column for the **OnPreExecute** and **OnPostExecute** events.

3. Click the **OK** button to close the **Set Breakpoints** dialog. You should now see a single breakpoint icon in your **Script Task**. The designer shows only one, even though two breakpoints have been set.

4. Press **F5** to execute the package, or select **Debug**⇨ **Start** from the Designer menu.

Almost immediately, you will hit the **OnPreExecute** breakpoint of your Script Task and package execution will pause. At this point, you can examine the system variable, *StartTime*, and your user variable, *DayOfWeek*, to see their current values. Do this using the **Locals** window that shows the current value of local variables. The following steps explain how. (You can see the **Locals** window in Figure 5.8.)

1. Show the **Locals** window by selecting **Debug**⇨ **Windows**⇨ **Locals** from the Designer menu, or with the key combination **Ctrl+Alt+V,L**.

2. Expand the **Variables** selection by clicking the plus sign (+) beside **Variables**. The expanded view shows all the system variables and any user variables that are visible to the task or object where the debugger hit the current breakpoint. You should be able to see the current value of **System:: StartTime**. This is the start time of the package.

3. Scroll through the list until you find **User::DayOfWeek**.

4. Expand the **DayOfWeek** node by clicking the plus sign beside it. The window will now show the **Type** and **CurrentValue** of the variable.

5. If you like, you can change the current value of the user variable by typing a new value in the **CurrentValue** row of the **Locals** window. This immediately changes the value of the variable in the package, although in this case we are not reading from this value.

Name	Value	Type
Variables		
System::CancelEvent	{6028}	Int32
System::CreationDate	{5/18/2005 10:06:22 PM}	DateTime
System::CreatorComputerName	{TESTBED_01}	String
System::CreatorName	{ TESTBED_01\Administrator }	String
User::DayOfWeek	{}	String
System::ExecutionInstanceGUID	{{FB02DF2D-F73C-4006-8431-4A03945148F0}}	String
System::InteractiveMode	{True}	Boolean
System::LocaleID	{1033}	Int32
System::MachineName	{TESTBED_01}	String
User::MasterCount	{0}	Int32
System::OfflineMode	{False}	Boolean
System::PackageID	{{6C3C89FD-15FC-4DD0-9584-E41700E2B3C3}}	String
System::PackageName	{Package}	String
System::StartTime	{5/18/2005 11:03:06 PM}	DateTime
System::UserName	{ TESTBED_01\Administrator }	String
System::VersionBuild	{9}	Int32

Figure 5.8: Locals Window.

You can *try* to change the value of the system variable too, but as soon as you attempt to confirm the change, the original value will return. System variables are, of course, read-only.

It is good to be able to examine local variables, but it would also be useful to watch them while the values change. This would help you see that your script is working correctly.

Do this by following these steps.

1. Select the **DayOfWeek** node in the **Locals** window.

2. Right-click and select **Add Watch** from the contextual menu.

3. A **Watch** window will appear, probably named **Watch 1**.

4. The **Watch** window shows the **DayOfWeek** user variable and its current value.

You can see the Watch window in Figure 5.9. Now you can watch the value of the user variable as it changes.

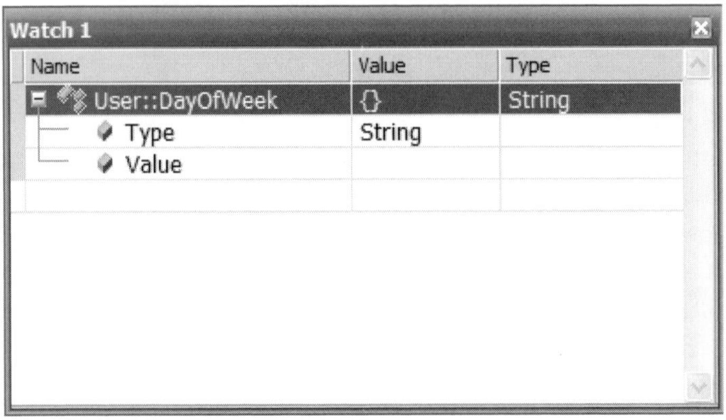
Watch 1
Name
Value
Type
User::DayOfWeek
{}
String
Type
String
Value

Figure 5.9: Watch Window.

To see this change, continue with the execution of the package by pressing **F5** or by selecting **Debug⇨Continue** from the Designer menu. The Script Task will execute, but you will not yet see it turn red or green. This is because it hits the **OnPostExecute** breakpoint first. However, you should be able to see that the **Watch** window correctly shows the current value of the *DayOfWeek* variable.

If you navigate to the **Locals** window, you should see the correct value there too. If you navigate to the **Breakpoints** window, you should see that the debugger has hit the OnPostExecute breakpoint.

Now continue package execution once more. The Script Task will turn red or green, depending on the day of the week on which the package started, and the **Package Execution Completed** message appears at the bottom of the Designer window.

TechTip:

Note that when the package completes debugging, and the Package Execution Completed message appears at the bottom of the Designer window, you can no longer examine variables. This is why it is often useful to add an OnPostExecute breakpoint to the package itself. It enables you to examine all variables at the end of the debugging process.

Debugging the Script

As you can see, it is very useful to be able to debug a package, to see current variables and to be able to watch them change. However, you can do more than this with a Script Task; you can also debug the script itself. In fact, you can add breakpoints within a script and step through it line by line, to see how it behaves and to examine the current values of variables within the script.

1. Double-click the **Script Task** to open the **Script Task Editor**.

2. On the **Script** tab, click the **Design Script** button.

3. In the script, find the following line of code:

    ```
    t = CDate(Dts.Variables("StartTime").Value).DayOfWeek.ToString
    ```

4. Right-click on this line of code. Select **Breakpoint**⇨ **Insert Breakpoint** from the contextual menu. A red dot will appear in the vertical grey bar to the left of the selected line. In the future, you can simply set a breakpoint by clicking here if you like.

5. You can also remove breakpoints by clicking the red dot that indicates a breakpoint, or by selecting **Breakpoint**⇨ **Delete Breakpoint** from the contextual menu of the line of code.

Figure 5.10 shows the script with a breakpoint added. Now you have set a breakpoint in your script, you should close the VSA environment and click the **OK** button to close the Script Task Editor. If you now examine the **Breakpoints** window of your package, you will notice that a new breakpoint has appeared. The Designer **Breakpoints** window knows about breakpoints inside the script!

```
ScriptMain                                                              ▾ ✕
ScriptMain                              ▾    ◆ Main                      ▾
⊟ Public Class ScriptMain                                                ▲

      ' The DTS execution engine calls this method when the task executes.
      ' To access the DTS object model, use the Dts object. Connections, variables,
      ' and logging features are available as static members of the Dts class.
      ' Before returning from this method, set the value of Dts.TaskResult to indica
      '
      ' To open Code and Text Editor Help, press F1.
      ' To open Object Browser, press Ctrl+Alt+J.

      Public Sub Main()
          '
          ' Add your code here
          '
●         Dim t As String
          t = CDate(Dts.Variables("StartTime").Value).DayOfWeek.ToString
          Dts.Variables("DayOfWeek").Value = t
          If t = "Saturday" Or t = "Sunday" Then
              Dts.TaskResult = Dts.Results.Failure
          Else
              Dts.TaskResult = Dts.Results.Success
          End If
      End Sub

 ⌊ End Class                                                              ▼
◄                         ⁞⁞⁞⁞                                          ►
```

Figure 5.10: Script with Breakpoint Added.

Having set a breakpoint in your script, you can remove all the other breakpoints in your package. Now we will execute the package and see what happens with a script breakpoint.

Press **F5** to execute the package, or select **Debug**⇨ **Start** from the Designer menu. Almost immediately after the package starts executing, the Script Task will execute and then the VSA environment will open. The script editor will show your selected line of code highlighted, and the breakpoint icon will have changed to a red dot with a yellow arrow. This shows that you have reached this point of the script. Figure 5.11 shows this line of code with the current breakpoint indicated.

```
ScriptMain                                                          ▾ ✕
ScriptMain                               ∨    ◆ Main                 ∨
  └ ' The ScriptMain class is the entry point of the Script Task.

  Imports System
  Imports System.Data
  Imports System.Math
  Imports Microsoft.SqlServer.Dts.Runtime

⊟ Public Class ScriptMain

⊟      ' The DTS execution engine calls this method when the task executes.
       ' To access the DTS object model, use the Dts object. Connections, variable
       ' and logging features are available as static members of the Dts class.
       ' Before returning from this method, set the value of Dts.TaskResult to in
       '
       ' To open Code and Text Editor Help, press F1.
       ' To open Object Browser, press Ctrl+Alt+J.

⊟      Public Sub Main()
           '
           ' Add your code here
           '
           Dim t As String
           t = CDate(Dts.Variables("StartTime").Value).DayOfWeek.ToString
           Dts.Variables("DayOfWeek").Value = t
           If t = "Saturday" Or t = "Sunday" Then
               Dts.TaskResult = Dts.Results.Failure
           Else
```

Figure 5.11: Hitting a Breakpoint in a Script.

The VSA environment has **Locals** and **Watches** windows, just like the main designer. You can experiment with these, just as you did with the windows in the designer, but you will notice an important difference. The only user variable you will see in this case is the variable *t*. This variable will hold the string value of the **DayOfWeek** function for use within the script. It is the only variable in the script environments **Locals** window, because *t* is the only variable used in the script. You cannot see package variables in the script designer and you cannot see script variables in the package designer.

One of the most useful debugging features of the script editor is the ability to *step into* a script line by line. To do this, you must have set a breakpoint in the script. Once the script hits the breakpoint, you can use the **F11** key (or **Debug⇨ Step Into** from the script Designer menu) to step through the script.

Another useful debugging feature is the ability to examine the current value of a variable (such as *t*) or an object property (such as `Dts.TaskResult`) simply by holding your mouse pointer over the relevant point in the script when you have hit a breakpoint. The current value will appear in a Tool Tip. Figure 5.12 shows the display of the script designer while stepping through a script.

```vb
' The ScriptMain class is the entry point of the Script Task.

Imports System
Imports System.Data
Imports System.Math
Imports Microsoft.SqlServer.Dts.Runtime

Public Class ScriptMain

    ' The DTS execution engine calls this method when the task executes.
    ' To access the DTS object model, use the Dts object. Connections, variable
    ' and logging features are available as static members of the Dts class.
    ' Before returning from this method, set the value of Dts.TaskResult to ind

    ' To open Code and Text Editor Help, press F1.
    ' To open Object Browser, press Ctrl+Alt+J.

    Public Sub Main()
        '
        ' Add your code here
        '
        Dim t As String
        t = CDate(Dts.Variables("StartTime").Value).DayOfWeek.ToString
        Dts.Variables("DayOfWeek").Value = t
        If t = "Saturday" Or t = "Sunday" Then
            Dts.TaskResult = Dts.Results.Failure
        Else
```

Figure 5.12: Stepping Through a Script.

When stepping through a script, if you get to the last line of the script and select to step in again, by pressing **F11**, you will see the following error: **There is no source code available for the current location**. This error simply means you have run out of script! Click the **OK** button in the error dialog, and then press **F5** to continue with the package. The script designer will close. You will return to the package designer, and package execution will continue.

Summary

Script Tasks can pass information to and from SSIS using variables.

Tracking the progress of a package and ensuring that scripts and variables are behaving as expected could be a complex process. However, debugging packages becomes easy when you use breakpoints in the package and even within the script itself.

This chapter has covered a lot of ground, but by now you should feel comfortable with the behavior of the Script Task in your packages. The ability able to script workflow operations in this way will enable you to drive quite complex processes from SSIS. In fact, I have often seen applications where architects used SSIS primarily as a workflow engine.

Workflow can be even more flexible when it embraces events, and when it can integrate very diverse operations. The next chapter will introduce some more advanced features to enable these requirements, including using events in scripts, and calling other .NET assemblies.

Did you know?

When connecting SSIS tasks or components, you usually drag a connector between them. However, you can also auto-connect shapes. Select **Tools→Options** from the main menu of the Designer. Expand the Business Intelligence Designers node in the tree view. There are options to auto-connect Control Flow and Data Flow. With auto-connect, you add new shapes to the package and they connect automatically. Simply select a shape on the design surface, then double-click in the toolbox to choose the next shape you want. SSIS will add it and connect the first shape to it.

Chapter 6

Advanced Uses of the Script Task

In this chapter, we will look at some other useful features of the Script Task, including logging and the ability to call other .NET assemblies.

Logging in SSIS

We have previously said that SSIS packages, and data integration processes in general, usually run unattended. In such circumstances, it is important that the application should generate detailed logs. Without good logs, administrators would be unable to track the execution of processes or to understand any errors that arose. To this end, SSIS provides wide-ranging logging capabilities.

SSIS performs its logging by writing log entries to *log providers* that in turn save the log entries to some form of data store. By default, you can log data to SQL Server, SQL Server Profiler, text files, XML files, and Microsoft Windows Event log. It is also possible for advanced developers to write their own log providers.

You can select to write out log entries for the package, and or for any task or container in the package. Packages can have multiple logs to different providers, too. In fact, logging in SSIS is so thorough that the details are beyond the scope of this book. For more information, you should consult the product documentation.

For your current needs, you will add some simple logging to your package, and write information to that log from within your script. To add a log to your package, follow these steps.

1. Select **SSIS**⇨ **Logging** from the Designer menu. The **Configure SSIS Logs** dialog box will appear, as shown in Figure 6.1.

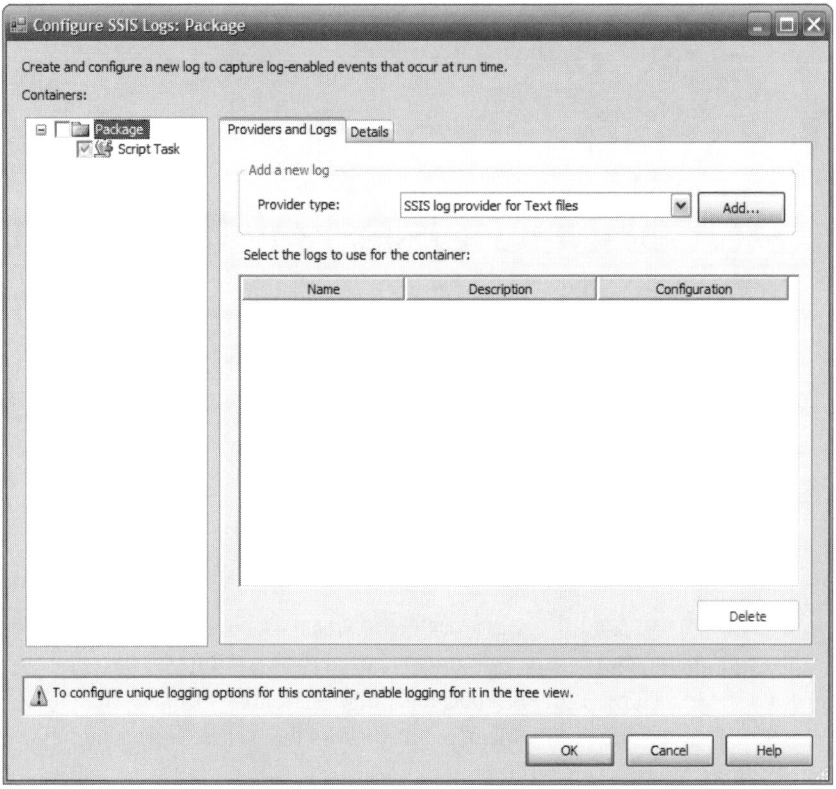

Figure 6.1: Configure SSIS Logs Dialog Box.

2. In the **Containers** view on the left, you will see a tree of the package and its tasks and containers. In this case, you will see the **Package** and the **Script Task**.

3. Check the check box for **Package**. This enables logging for the package itself. You should see that the logging dialog grays out the **Script Task** and checks it by default. This means that the **Script Task** will inherit all the options you set for logging the package. This is a useful default setting.

4. On the right-hand side of the dialog box, on the **Providers and Logs** tab, select a log provider from the **Provider type** list, then click the **Add** button. For this example, select **SSIS Log provider for XML files**. The dialog will add an entry for this provider to the list box on the **Providers and Logs** tab.

5. Check the entry for this provider in the list box. In the **Configuration** column, select <**New connection**> from the drop-down list. As soon as you confirm the choice of <**New connection**> (either by pressing **Enter** or by navigating to another object) the **File Connection Manager Editor** will prompt you for a file connection (see Figure 6.2).

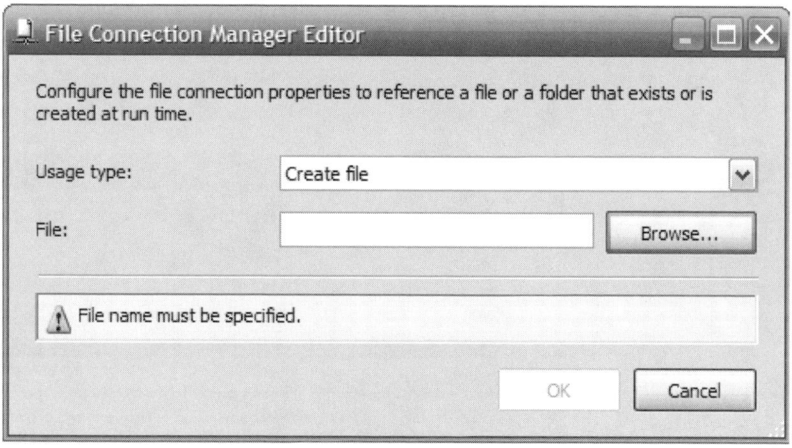

Figure 6.2: File Connection Manager Editor.

6. Select **Create file** from the **Usage type** list. Click the **Browse** button and navigate to a suitable folder. Enter the file name of the log file you wish to create: MyLog.xml, for example. Click the **OK** button to close the **File Connection Manager Editor**.

7. Back at the **Configure SSIS Logs** dialog box, select the **Details** tab. On this tab, you will select the events to log. You should recognize these events—they are the same events on which you could add a breakpoint.

8. Check the box beside each event you wish to log. As a minimum, it is good practice to select **OnError**, **OnWarning**, and **OnTaskFailed**. If you would like to see when individual tasks started and stopped, check the **OnPreExecute** and **OnPostExecute** events. **OnInformation** is useful because some tasks write additional information about their activities here. Check this event, because we will use this in our script.

At this stage, the dialog box will look like the example in Figure 6.3.

Tech Tip:

Once you complete these steps, you will notice that a Connection Manager for the log file connection has appeared in the **Connection Managers** area. If you edit the connection string on this Connection Manager, then SSIS will save the log to the new location you specify. You do not need to change anything in the logging dialog. This is one of the advantages of Connection Managers—they decouple connections from the objects that use them.

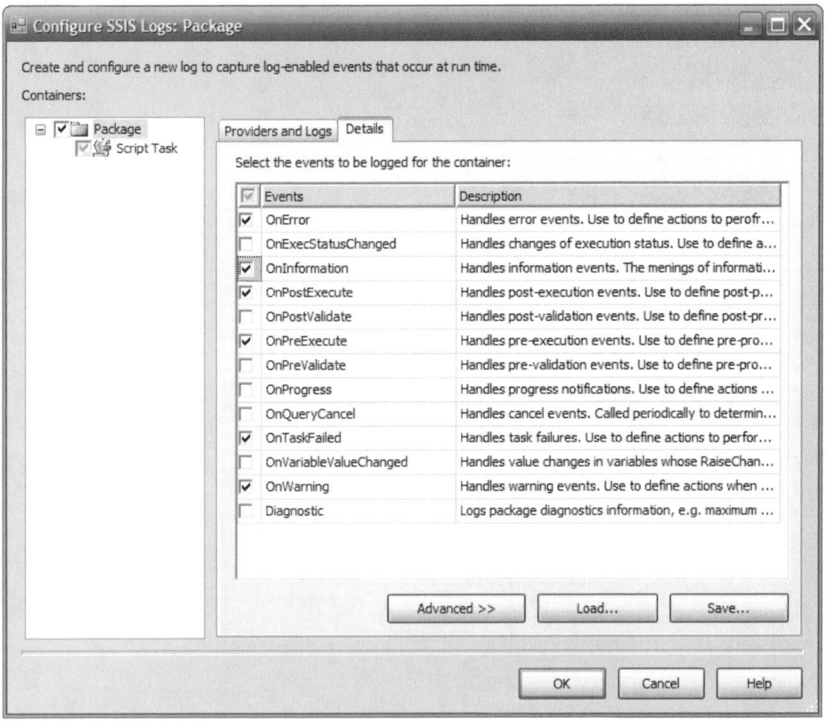

Figure 6.3: Configure SSIS Logs Dialog Box with Selected Events.

9. You can now click the **OK** button to close the **Configure SSIS Logs** dialog.

If you were to execute the package now, you would see a number of log records describing the execution of the package. For example, Listing 6.1 shows the record for the **PackageStart** event.

```
<record>
        <event>PackageStart</event>
        <message>Beginning of package execution.</message>
        <computer>DFARMER1</computer>
        <operator>MYDOMAIN\dfarmer</operator>
        <source>Package</source>
        <sourceid>{DD19BDD4-FAD9-46E6-B090-219ABD052DB1}</sourceid>
        <executionid>{457E86DF-B0DA-4C3A-AB07-4411CBC1AD6D}</executionid>
        <starttime>5/1/2005 9:44:38 PM</starttime>
        <endtime>5/1/2005 9:44:38 PM</endtime>
        <datacode>0</datacode>
        <databytes>0x</databytes>
</record>
```

Listing 6.1: XML Log Record for the PackageStart Event.

You can see from this record that SSIS logs some very useful information by default, including the source of the event (in this case, the package) and the computer and operator name. The records in Listing 6.2 show that the script task raised an error and that it failed, because the package executed on the weekend.

```
<record>
        <event>OnError</event>
        <message>The Script returned a failure result.</message>
        <computer>DFARMER1</computer>
        <operator>MYDOMAIN\dfarmer</operator>
        <source>Package</source>
        <sourceid>{DD19BDD4-FAD9-46E6-B090-219ABD052DB1}</sourceid>
        <executionid>{457E86DF-B0DA-4C3A-AB07-4411CBC1AD6D}</executionid>
        <starttime>5/8/2005 9:44:39 PM</starttime>
        <endtime>5/8/2005 9:44:39 PM</endtime>
        <datacode>4</datacode>
        <databytes>0x</databytes>
</record>
<record>
        <event>OnTaskFailed</event>
        <message>(null)</message>
        <computer>DFARMER1</computer>
```

```
                <operator>MYDOMAIN\dfarmer</operator>
                <source>Scheduling Script</source>
                <sourceid>{31E1139E-EDE4-493C-A753-4E08D101FA3D}</sourceid>
                <executionid>{457E86DF-B0DA-4C3A-AB07-4411CBC1AD6D}</executionid>
                <starttime>5/8/2005 9:44:39 PM</starttime>
                <endtime>5/8/2005 9:44:39 PM</endtime>
                <datacode>0</datacode>
                <databytes>0x</databytes>
      </record>
```

Listing 6.2: XML Log Entries Showing a Task Failure.

It is possible to write directly to the SSIS log from within your script. However, as you can see from the example above, SSIS logs events anyway if you select them in the **Configure SSIS Logs** dialog box. Events allow for even greater flexibility and are a useful advanced feature of SSIS. In Chapter 2, you read a brief description of event handling in SSIS. Event handlers enable the SSIS runtime engine to execute sequences of tasks on an event, rather than by using a precedence constraint from a task. For all these reasons, you may find it a better practice to raise events in your script, and to log these events.

The next section shows how to add these events to your script.

Adding Events to a Script

Now we can edit our script to add our own details to SSIS events. Listing 6.3 shows a version of Sub Main() that includes code to raise events about our script through the **OnInformation** event. Because we have selected to log **OnInformation** events, SSIS will also write these messages to the log file.

```
Public Sub Main()
      '
      ' Add your code here
      '
      Dim t As String
      t = CDate(Dts.Variables("StartTime").Value).DayOfWeek.ToString
      Dts.Variables("DayOfWeek").Value = t
      If t = "Saturday" Or t = "Sunday" Then
            Dts.Events.FireInformation(1, "", _
                "Package started during the weekend.", "", 0, True)
```

```
              Dts.TaskResult = Dts.Results.Failure
        Else
              Dts.Events.FireInformation(2, "", _
                  "Package started during the week.", "", 0, True)
              Dts.TaskResult = Dts.Results.Success
        End If
End Sub
```

Listing 6.3: Firing Events from Script.

As its name suggests, the **FireInformation** method raises an **OnInformation** event. The event model for SSIS is quite detailed, but you should be aware of the following parameters:

▶ **informationCode** — An integer to identify the message you are raising. In this script, there is a value of 1 for a weekend execution, and 2 for a weekday execution.

▶ **subComponent** — A string that can contain more details about the object raising the event. In this script, the value is as an empty string. This is because the log does not report this value. If you were using this event in a package with event handlers, you might use the value to include additional details of the event.

▶ **description** — This string is reported by the default log, so this script example sets it to a useful description for each case: `Package started during the weekend` or `Package started during the week`.

▶ **helpFile** — This string is the path to a Help file which could include documentation of this event. This sample does not use this value, so it is an empty string.

▶ **helpContext** — An integer which would represent the Help context for this message in the Help file, if used. In this case, it is simply 0, because the value is not used.

▶ **fireAgain** — This Boolean value tells the runtime whether to continue raising this event or to suppress subsequent instances of it for this execution. It is useful for events that may be expensive to process. In this case, it can be `True`.

If you execute the package with these changes to the script, the messages in Listing 6.4 will appear in the log. You will see that it is quite easy to relate the log to the **OnInformation** event that you raised. However, notice that there are two events in this listing, not just one. Why is this? You can find the answer in the <source> element for each event—the Scheduling Script component raised one, and the Package containing the script raised the other.

```
<record>
        <event>OnInformation</event>
        <message>Package started during the weekend.</message>
        <computer>HUTCHESON</computer>
        <operator>REDMOND\dfarmer</operator>
        <source>Scheduling Script</source>
        <sourceid>{31E1139E-EDE4-493C-A753-4E08D101FA3D}</sourceid>
        <executionid>{F4A57A1D-E9BC-489A-A2C7-C284707FF6C5}</executionid>
        <starttime>5/8/2005 10:00:21 PM</starttime>
        <endtime>5/8/2005 10:00:21 PM</endtime>
        <datacode>1</datacode>
        <databytes>0x</databytes>
</record>
<record>
        <event>OnInformation</event>
        <message>Package started during the weekend.</message>
        <computer>HUTCHESON</computer>
        <operator>REDMOND\dfarmer</operator>
        <source>Package</source>
        <sourceid>{DD19BDD4-FAD9-46E6-B090-219ABD052DB1}</sourceid>
        <executionid>{F4A57A1D-E9BC-489A-A2C7-C284707FF6C5}</executionid>
        <starttime>5/8/2005 10:00:21 PM</starttime>
        <endtime>5/8/2005 10:00:21 PM</endtime>
        <datacode>1</datacode>
        <databytes>0x</databytes>
</record>
```

Listing 6.4: XML Log Entries Raised by the Script in Listing 6.3.

From within your script, you can use the following methods for different events:

► FireCustomEvent

► FireError

► FireInformation

► FireProgress

► FireQueryCancel

► FireWarning

Tech Tip:

It is quite easy to log directly from within your script instead of using events. The syntax is simply:

```
Dts.Log( messageText As String, dataCode As Integer,
dataBytes As Byte() )
```

You will most likely not wish to pass any special values for the dataCode and dataBytes parameters. You can simply pass in 0 as the dataCode. For the dataBytes, it is best to create a local variable of Byte type simply to provide a value to pass, such as:

```
Dim placeholderBytes(0) As Byte
```

Therefore, to write a line to the log, you could use the following call:

```
Dts.Log("My log message", 0, placeholderBytes )
```

Using .NET Assemblies with SSIS

The ability to reference .NET assemblies through VSA scripts is one of the most exciting features of SSIS. It enables easy integration of code directly in your processes from three important sources:

▶ The full library of the .NET Framework

▶ Code libraries from Microsoft and third parties, shipped as .NET assemblies

▶ Your own custom assemblies containing business rules or code for reuse over many SSIS packages (and perhaps with other applications throughout your enterprise)

You can write your own custom assemblies in any .NET language, and languages such as COBOL, Lisp, and Perl are available in .NET versions. In fact, NET supports over twenty languages. Therefore, there are many possibilities for integrating existing code directly with SSIS.

Leveraging the .NET Framework Library

This section shows a simple example of extending SSIS with the .NET Framework Library. In addition, you will learn how to use the Script Task with one of the most useful container objects in SSIS—the ForEach Loop.

You may be aware already of the SSIS File System Task. This useful task can perform numerous file operations including setting attribute flags. However, the File System Task does not support *reading* the attribute flags. In this sample, the script will use the .NET Framework **System.IO** Namespace and the **File** class, to read the attributes of a file into a variable.

Adding a ForEachLoop to Your Package

Use these steps to add a ForEach Loop to a package:

1. Create a new package in the BI Development Studio.

2. Drag a **ForEach Loop** from the **Toolbox** to the **Control Flow** design surface.

3. Double-click the **ForEach Loop** shape on the design surface to open the **ForEach Loop Editor** dialog box.

4. On the **General** tab, you can rename the loop and add a description if you like. It is always useful to add meaningful names and descriptions for later usability.

5. Click **Collection** in the list view on the left to move to the **Collection** tab.

6. Select the **For Each File enumerator** (the type of collection over which you shall loop) from the **Enumerator** list. In fact, this should be the default unless you have some custom enumerators installed.

7. Browse for the **Folder** that contains the files you wish to enumerate. You can also define the filenames you wish to loop over using wildcards, the extent of the filespec, and whether to loop over subfolders. Figure 6.4 shows the **ForEach Loop Editor** configured at this stage.

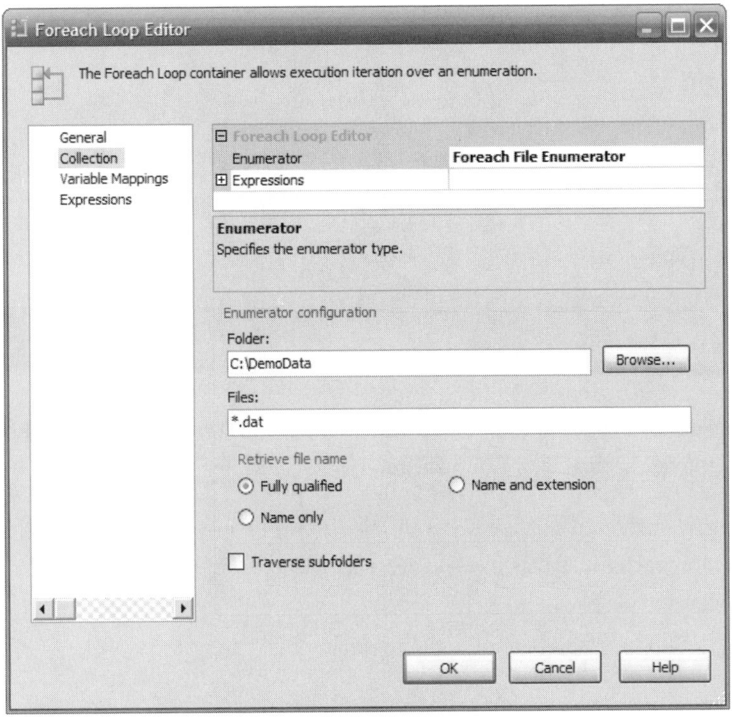

Figure 6.4: ForEach Loop Editor Configured to Enumerate Files.

8. Click **Variable Mappings** to move to the **Variable Mappings** tab.

9. In the grid, select <**New Variable**> from the drop-down list in the **Variable** column. The **Add Variable** dialog box will appear.

10. In the **Add Variable** dialog box, rename the new variable `CurrentFileName`, but leave its data type as **String** and its default value as empty.

11. Click the **OK** button to close the **Add Variable** dialog box. Figure 6.5 shows the **Add Variable** dialog box configured for a new variable.

![Add Variable dialog box]

Add Variable

Specify the properties of the new variable.

Container:	Package
Name:	CurrentFileName
Namespace:	User
Value type:	String
Value:	
☐ Read only	

OK   Cancel

Figure 6.5: Add Variable Dialog Box.

12. You do not need to update the **Index** column. You can now click the **OK** button on the **ForEach Loop Editor**.

You have now configured a loop to iterate over the files in your selected folder. As the loop enumerates each file, it sets the selected variable to the current value of the loop—the current filename.

Adding Objects to the Loop

Now it is time to add a variable that will hold the attributes of the current file:

1. Ensure that the **ForEach Loop** is selected in the **Control Flow** designer.

2. If you cannot see the **Variables** window, select **SSIS**⇨ **Variables** from the Designer menu. You should be able to see the **CurrentFileName** variable already in this window.

3. In the **Variables** window, click the **New Variable** button to create a new variable. You will notice that the variable scope is the **ForEach Loop**. This variable can only be seen by the loop and objects within the loop. This is because the loop was the selected objected when you clicked **New Variable**. SSIS created the variable in the loop.

4. This new variable will be of type **Int32** by default. Change its **Data Type** to String. Ensure the default value is empty.

5. Rename the variable to Attributes.

Having added a variable to hold the result, you should now use the following steps to add the Script Task and configure it to use the variables we have created.

1. Drag a **Script Task** from the **Toolbox** to the **Control Flow** design surface.

2. Drop the **Script Task** within the loop shape.

3. Double-click the **Script Task** to open the **Script Task Editor**.

4. Give the **Script Task** a useful **Name** and **Description** on the **General** tab.

5. Click **Script** to move to the **Script** tab.

6. Enter CurrentFileName as the value of the **ReadOnlyVariables** property. You will read from this variable in the script, but not write to it.

7. Enter Attributes as the value of the **ReadWriteVariables** property. You will write back to this variable in the script.

8. Now click **Design Script** to open the script editor.

Listing 6.5 shows the script that you should create in the script editor.

```vb
Imports System
Imports System.Data
Imports System.Math
Imports Microsoft.SqlServer.Dts.Runtime
Imports System.IO


Public Class ScriptMain
    Public Sub Main()
        'Declare a variable to hold the attributes
        Dim a As FileAttributes

        'Declare a variable to hold the attributes as a string
        Dim atts As String

        a = File.GetAttributes(Dts.Variables("CurrentFileName").Value.ToString)

        If (a And FileAttributes.Archive) = _
            FileAttributes.Archive Then
            atts = "A"
        End If

        If (a And FileAttributes.Compressed) = _
            FileAttributes.Compressed Then
            atts = atts + "C"
        End If

        If (a And FileAttributes.Encrypted) = _
            FileAttributes.Encrypted Then
            atts = atts + "E"
        End If

        If (a And FileAttributes.Hidden) = _
            FileAttributes.Hidden Then
            atts = atts + "H"
```

```
        End If

        If (a And FileAttributes.ReadOnly) = _
                FileAttributes.ReadOnly Then
            atts = atts + "R"
        End If

        If (a And FileAttributes.System) = _
                FileAttributes.System Then
            atts = atts + "S"
        End If

        Dts.Variables("Attributes").Value = atts

        Dts.TaskResult = Dts.Results.Success
    End Sub
End Class
```

Listing 6.5: Script to Get File Attributes.

Note that the script includes an **Imports** statement to import the **System.IO** namespace. This is not strictly necessary, but it does make reading and writing the script much easier. Without it, every reference to classes in that namespace would need to be fully qualified. For example, System.IO.File.GetAttributes(f).

You should now add a breakpoint to the Script Task (not to the script) on the **PostExecute** event. When you execute the package, you can open the **Locals** window and perhaps even add a Watch to the *CurrentFileName* and *Attributes* variables. See Chapter 5 if you need to jog your memory on how to do this. As the ForEach Loop iterates over your files, you will see the current file and its attributes reflected in the values of those variables.

Finally, you could use the *Attributes* variable in some way. For example, you could add a File System Task to the loop to move the file to another folder. A common scenario would be to constrain the second task to execute only if the Archive flag is set. You would do this by adding an expression to the precedence constraint between the Script Task and the second task.

Add the **File System Task** and expression as follows:

1. Drag a **File System Task** shape from the **Toolbox** to the **ForEach Loop** and drop it within the loop.

2. Connect a precedence constraint from the **Script Task** to the **File System Task**.

3. Double-click the precedence constraint to open the **Precedence Constraint Editor**.

4. Select **Expression and Constraint** as the **Evaluation Operation**. The second task will now only execute if first task succeeds *and* if the expression is true.

5. Edit the **Expression** to read FINDSTRING(@Attributes,"A", 1) > 0

6. Click the **OK** button to close the **Precedence Constraint Editor**.

This expression returns True if the value of the *Attributes* variable contains the letter "A" for the archive flag. Figure 6.6 shows the **Precedence Constraint Editor**.

Precedence Constraint Editor

A precedence constraint defines the workflow between two executables. The precedence constraint can be based on a combination of the execution results and the evaluation of expressions.

Constraint options

Evaluation operation:	Expression and Constraint
Value:	Success
Expression:	FINDSTRING(@Attributes,"A", 1) > 0 [Test]

Multiple constraints

If the constrained task has multiple constraints, you can choose how the constraints interoperate to control the execution of the constrained task.

- ⦿ Logical AND. All constraints must evaluate to True
- ○ Logical OR. One constraint must evaluate to True

[OK] [Cancel] [Help]

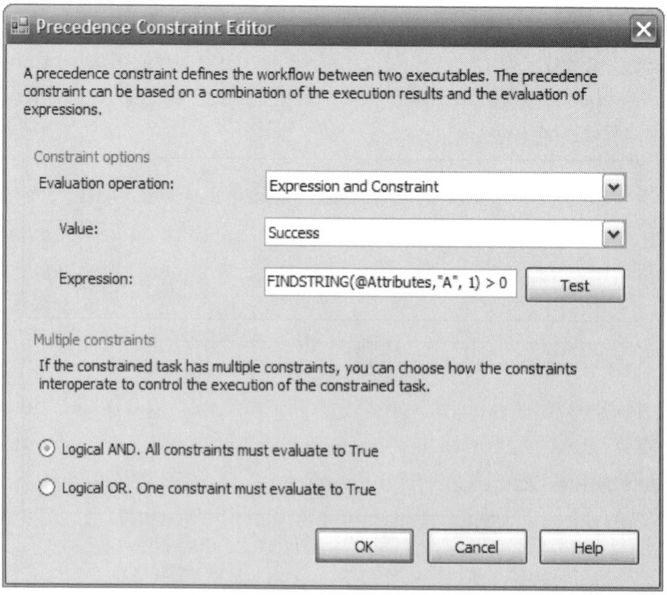

Figure 6.6: Precedence Constraint Editor.

To configure the **File System Task**, follow these steps:

1.   Double-click the **File System Task** to open the **File System Task Editor**.

2.   Give the **File System Task** a useful **Name** and **Description** on the **General** tab.

3.   Set the **Operation** property to **Move File**.

4.   The **Source Connection** properties describe where the file is coming from. Set **IsSourcePathVariable** to True, because the file name will come from the current value of the ForEach loop enumerator that is stored in the **CurrentFileName** variable.

5.   The **SourceConnection** property changes to **SourceVariable**. Select CurrentFileName from the drop-down list for this property.

6.   Now you need to use the **DestinationConnection** properties to set a destination folder for the files that the task will move.

7.   Leave **IsDestinationPathVariable** False.

8.   For the **DestinationConnection** property, select <**New Connection**> from the drop-down list. The editor will show the **File Connection Manager Editor** that you saw earlier in Figure 6.2.

9.   Select **Existing Folder** as the **Usage Type**, and use the **Browse** button to select a folder to which you will move the archived files.

Now you are ready to run the package. The ForEach Loop will enumerate files in your selected folder. The script will get the attributes and create a string list of them in the *Attributes* variable. If the attributes for a file include "A" (the archive flag), then the File System Task will move the file to your selected destination folder.

⚠ *Caution:*

When you run this package, the File System Task will move files from one folder to another. Therefore, be sure to specify folders that are safe to work with in this way.

Leveraging Other Assemblies

In addition to making the .NET Framework available for your data integration projects, SSIS can also use other assemblies.

In order for SSIS to use an assembly, it must be in a folder where SSIS can reference it.

This folder is located here:

```
<windows>\Microsoft.NET\Framework\v2.0.<build#>
```

Where `<windows>` is your Windows folder (typically `c:\windows`) and `<build#>` is the specific build of .NET Framework 2.0. If you have more than one build folder for the Framework, choose the highest number.

In this section, you will add a very simple script that uses a SQL Server Analysis Services assembly to check for a local Analysis Server and returns the number of databases found there. For this script to work, you must have Analysis Services installed. However, even if you cannot build this sample yourself, the basic principles of using other assemblies should be clear.

Before using the assembly in a script, first follow these steps:

1. Create a new SSIS package.

2. Add a **Script Task** to the **Control Flow** design surface.

3. Add a new **Variable** with an **Int32** data type. Name it `DatabaseCount`.

Adding the Assembly Reference

The first step is to ensure the assembly is present in the folder where SSIS can reference it. For your Analysis Services script, the assembly to copy will be in this folder:

```
C:\Program Files\Microsoft SQL Server\90\SDK\Assemblies\
```

There are a number of assemblies here. You can experiment with them later! For now, copy the **Microsoft.AnalysisServices.dll** file to the .NET Framework folder mentioned previously.

Now we can set up the Script Task by using these steps:

1. Double-click the **Script Task** shape in the **Control Flow** to open the **Script Task Editor**.

2. As usual, give the task a useful **Name** and **Description** on the **General** tab..

3. On the **Script** tab, add `DatabaseCount` to the **ReadWriteVariables** property.

4. Click **Design Script** to open the VSA script environment.

5. Select **Project**⇨ **Add Reference** from the main menu of the VSA script environment. The **Add Reference** dialog box shown in Figure 6.7 will appear.

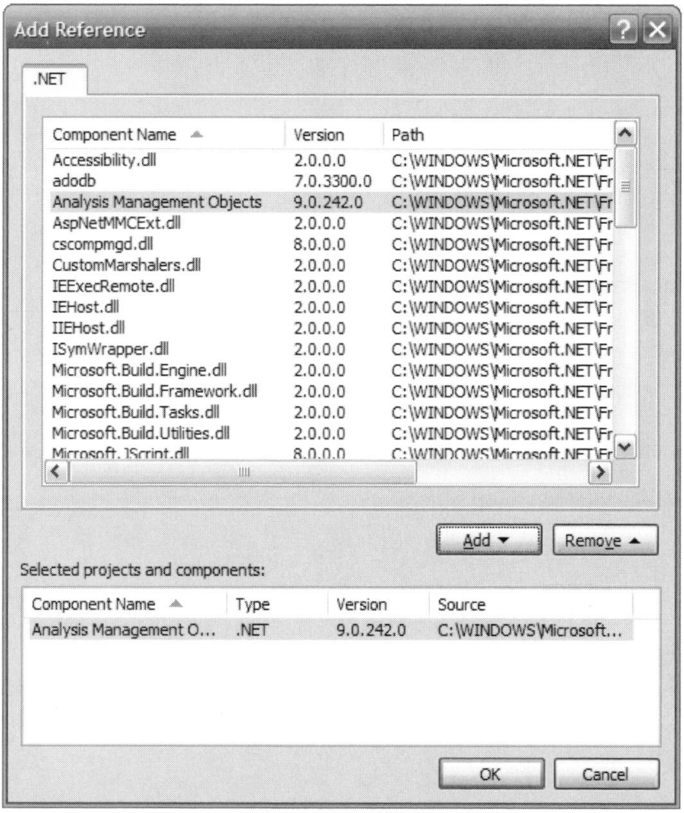

Figure 6.7: Add Reference Dialog Box.

6. In this dialog box, select the assembly named **Analysis Management Objects**. Developers often refer to this assembly as AMO, for short.

7. Click the **Add** button.

8. Click the **OK** button to close the dialog box and return to the script.

A reference to the Analysis Services assembly now exists in your project and is ready for use. You can check this by selecting **View⇨ Project Explorer** from the main menu of the VSA script environment. The **Project Explorer** window shown in Figure 6.8 will appear. Expand **References** to see your project references. You can also add and remove assembly references using this window.

Figure 6.8: Project Explorer Window.

Finally, edit the script to match the sample in Listing 6.6.

```
Imports System
Imports System.Data
Imports System.Math
Imports Microsoft.SqlServer.Dts.Runtime
Imports Microsoft.AnalysisServices


Public Class ScriptMain
```

```
Public Sub Main()
    Dim AS_Server As New Microsoft.AnalysisServices.Server
    Try
        AS_Server.Connect("localhost")
        Dts.Variables("DatabaseCount").Value = _
        AS_Server.Databases.Count
        Dts.TaskResult = Dts.Results.Success
    Catch e As Exception
        Dts.Events.FireError(0, e.Message, _"AS Server Check Script",   "",
        ⊃0)
        Dts.TaskResult = Dts.Results.Failure
    Finally
        AS_Server.Disconnect()
    End Try
End Sub
End Class
```

Listing 6.6: Script to Check for a Local Analysis Server.

As you can see, this is a very simple script indeed, yet it calls functions in a very powerful assembly. AMO gives you access to all the management functionality of Analysis Services. The first addition to the script is to import the assembly:

```
Imports Microsoft.AnalysisServices.
```

As you know, this is a convenience (but a very great one) when you come to call methods in the assembly. Next, we declare a variable to hold a new Server object.

```
Dim AS_Server As New Microsoft.AnalysisServices.Server
```

The script next uses a `Try … Catch … Finally … End Try` block to attempt to connect to the local Analysis Server. Note that the connection string is simply `"localhost"` to attempt a connection to a local server. In more advanced cases you would use an SSIS connection. Connections in scripts are described in more detail in Chapter 9. In the Finally block, the script ensures that the server is disconnected.

If the script can connect to the server, the number of databases is returned to the variable, and the Script Task will succeed. If the script cannot connect, then the Script Task will fail by setting the result to `Failure` in the `Catch` block. Notice that the script also fires an error event to give more information on the failure. This event could be captured in the log, or viewed in the **Progress** pane or **Output** window during debugging.

FREE *Bonus:*

If you register this book at www.rationalpress.com, you can download Bonus Chapter C, which describes how to leverage Web services throughout the data flow using script and .NET assemblies. This is a remarkably powerful scenario that enables SSIS to work in distributed service-oriented architectures.

Summary

When you have built an SSIS package, it is important to be able to log its execution in order to pick up errors or problems that may occur in production. Fortunately, SSIS has comprehensive logging features, and you can even add your own events to these.

Adding your own events is only one aspect of the extensibility of SSIS.

Another important feature is the ability to integrate functionality from .NET assemblies directly into your script tasks, and thus into your package workflow.

This level of integration with the .NET Framework and assemblies from within scripts is one of the most powerful features of SSIS. You will surely find many uses for these abilities in your work. However, remember that in Chapter 2 we said that the primary use of SSIS was to move data. In the next chapter, you will learn how to use the Script Component in the Data Flow, to bring the power of scripting to that scenario.

Script Components

Chapter 7

Your First Script Component

In Chapter 2, you learned about the three types of Data Flow components in SSIS: sources, transformations and destinations. This chapter describes these different types and show you how to create your first transformation component using script. Once you have mastered the Script Component, you will find that you can readily integrate almost any functionality into the SSIS Data Flow. Custom scripted data sources can handle otherwise unsupported file formats; custom transformations can call functions in managed assemblies, including the .NET Framework; and custom scripted destinations enable SSIS to output data in very flexible ways. In fact, it is quite possible to write sophisticated data flows for ETL and data integration using only script components!

Script Component Types

You will typically use script somewhat differently in each of the three component types.

Script Source Component

Source components have no input columns, but do have output columns. The purpose of the Script Component in this case is to deliver data to the output columns. For example, the component author could write a script using file and string handling functions to parse a complex text file whose format is not suitable for parsing with the Flat File Connection Manager.

Script Transformation Component

Transformation components have input columns and output columns. In these components, the script typically will transform the data in some way between inputs and outputs. What these transformations are is up to you—that is why scripts are so flexible. Chapter 2 discussed two different patterns of transformation: *synchronous* and *asynchronous*. Script components can handle both patterns quite easily.

A *synchronous* component, you will remember, is particularly useful for row-by-row transformations. For example, I may have incoming data that includes customer names. Perhaps for easy cross-referencing with other customer records, I would like to calculate a SOUNDEX value for each customer name. SOUNDEX is an algorithm invented by the US Census for codifying names to take account of different spellings. T-SQL has a SOUNDEX function, but SSIS does not.

An SSIS developer can code a SOUNDEX function in Visual Basic .NET script. With this, the script can transform every incoming customer name and emit a SOUNDEX value at the output.

> ### Note:
>
> SOUNDEX is an algorithm for matching strings (principally personal names) phonetically. Researchers have been using SOUNDEX since the 1880 US Census to conform different spellings of surnames in census reports to a standard value. For example, Smith and Smyth have the same SOUNDEX value. SOUNDEX helped researchers using Census data to match and find surnames, even with different spellings. The algorithm converts a name to a code where the first letter of the code is the first letter of the name, and a sequence of numbers represents the other syllables. SOUNDEX ignores vowels, double consonants and the letters Y, H and W. Therefore, in SOUNDEX, Alan and Allen both become A45. Alonso becomes A452.

An *asynchronous* component is useful for performing operations which change the shape of the data significantly, or where incoming rows do not have related rows at the output. A good use of an asynchronous script would be to aggregate text. The SSIS Aggregate component is very powerful, but it can only perform Min and Max calculations against numeric columns. If you need to be able to calculate the Min and Max values of a string column, this can easily be achieved in Visual Basic .NET script, as we shall see in Chapter 8.

Script Destination Component

As mentioned previously, it is possible to have a text file that the Flat File Connection Manager cannot parse, but which a script source component can handle. In an enterprise where text files like this are important to legacy applications, you may also need the ability to *write* data to a file in this format for the legacy application to read. The script destination component is useful in these circumstances. You will have guessed by now that a script destination component has input columns but no output columns. Instead, the Visual Basic .NET script handles the data, perhaps using file and string routines from the .NET Framework to output text files in the appropriate format.

Adding a Script Component to Your Package

The first Script Component we are going to look at it is a transformation component. In fact, we are going to build a simple SOUNDEX component to transform a column containing a name to a codified value representing the sound of the name, just as the US Census would do. As this first component is a transformation, it requires some data to work with. We can quickly build a package containing a Data Flow and a source component to get started.

> *Note:*
>
> This chapter assumes you have at least some familiarity with building a Data Flow with SSIS. You should at least be familiar with the simplest examples from the documentation or the samples that ship with the product.

Preparing the Package

Use the following steps to prepare the package:

1. Create a new SSIS package.

2. In the Designer, drag a **Data Flow Task** from the **Control Flow Items** tab of the **Toolbox** to the **Control Flow** design surface.

3. Double-click the **Data Flow Task** to open the **Data Flow** design surface.

4. Drag an **OLE DB Source** component from the **Data Flow Sources** tab of the **Toolbox**.

5. Double-click the **OLE DB Source** component shape on the design surface to open the **OLE DB Source Editor**.

6. Click the **New** button to create a new **OLE DB Connection Manager**.

7. Select an existing connection to your AdventureWorksDW database, or create a new one now. This assumes you have installed the sample databases with SQL Server.

8. Click the **OK** button to return to the **OLE DB Source Editor**.

9. Select the **Table or View Data Access Mode**.

10. Select the `[dbo].[DimCustomer]` table. (`DimCustomer` stands for Customer *Dimension* and is not a reflection on the intelligence of AdventureWorks customers! DimEmployee, however, may be a different matter.)

11. Click the **Preview** button if you would like to see the data in this table. Note the **Last Name** field that we shall be using later.

12. Click the **OK** button to close the **OLE DB Source Editor**.

Now we have some source data to work with. At this stage, your package design should look like the example in Figure 7.1.

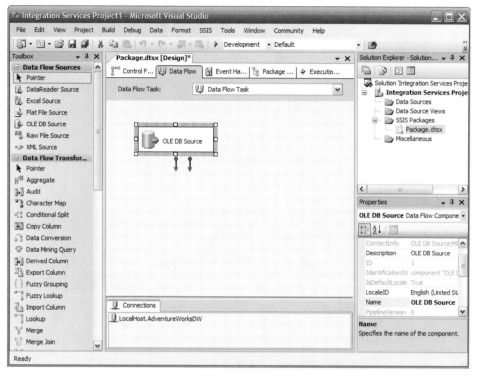

Figure 7.1: Package to Which We Will Add Our First Script Component.

Adding the Script Component

1. In the Designer, drag a **Script Component** from the **Data Flow Transformations** tab of the **Toolbox** to the **Data Flow** design surface.

2. When you drag the **Script Component**, the **Select Script Component Type Dialog** will appear, prompting you to select the kind of component you want to create (see Figure 7.2). This is important, as the configuration of the **Script Component** is somewhat different for each type. This dialog box sets up the component for you automatically, saving some work in creating this configuration yourself.

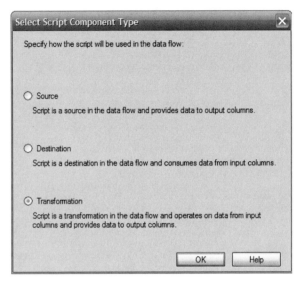

Figure 7.2: Select Component Type Dialog Box.

3. Select **Transformation** (the default) and click the **OK** button.

4. Now connect the output of the **OLE DB Source** to the **Script Component**. At this stage your package should look like Figure 7.3. Note the warning icon that appears in the **Script Component**. You can mouse over that to see the text of the warning. In this case, we have not yet added any script code, so the component at this point is in an invalid state.

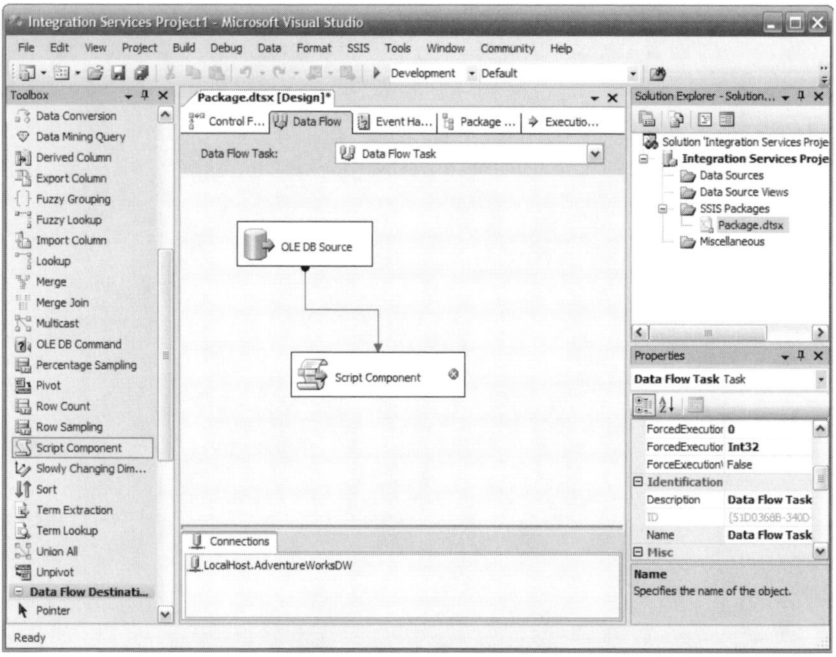

Figure 7.3: Package with OLE DB Source and Script Component Connected.

Adding Columns to Your Script Component

The next step is to tell your Script Component which input columns to work with. The Script Component requires you explicitly to say *in advance* which columns are required. This is because the component creates a wrapper that exposes these columns to the scripting environment. It would be expensive and redundant to expose all the input columns by default when you may only be using one of them.

Selecting the input columns is easy. Just follow these steps:

1. Double-click the **Script Component** shape on the design surface to open the **Script Transformation Editor**.

2. The default view is of the **Input Columns** tab. In this case, check the box next to the **Last Name** column. The component editor should now look like Figure 7.4.

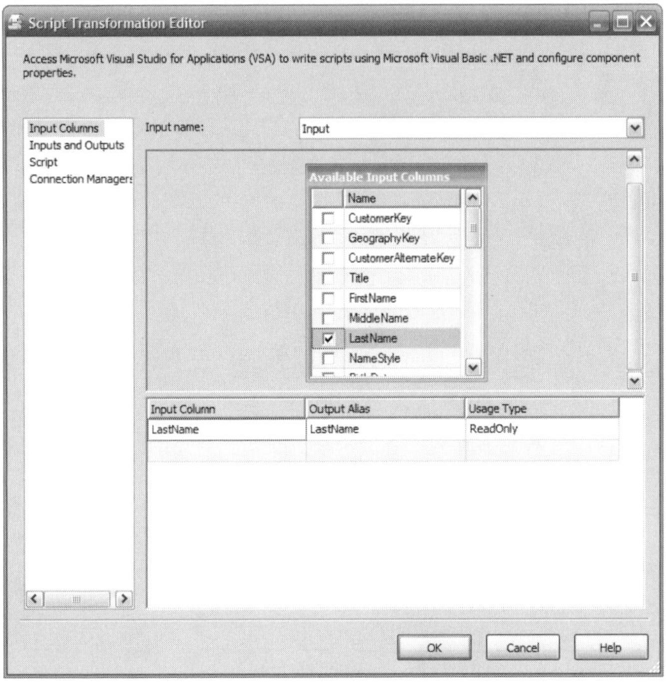

Figure 7.4: Component Editor with Last Name Column Selected.

Now we can use the **Last Name** column in our component. Note that we have left the **Usage Type** of the column as **Read Only**. This is because we do not want to *alter* the last name. Instead, we want to calculate a new column from the values in this column. But where will these new values go? We need to create a new column to hold these new values. This new column will not appear at the input. It is being calculated by the script, so it can only appear at the output.

We should add an Output Column, as follows:

1. Select the **Inputs and Outputs** tab of the **Script Transformation Editor**.

2. Expand the **Output** node of the **Inputs and Outputs** tree view.

3. Select the **Output Columns** folder under the **Output** node.

4. Click the **Add Column** button. This will add a new **Output Column**, named **Column** by default. The data type will be a four-byte signed integer. You can see this in Figure 7.5.

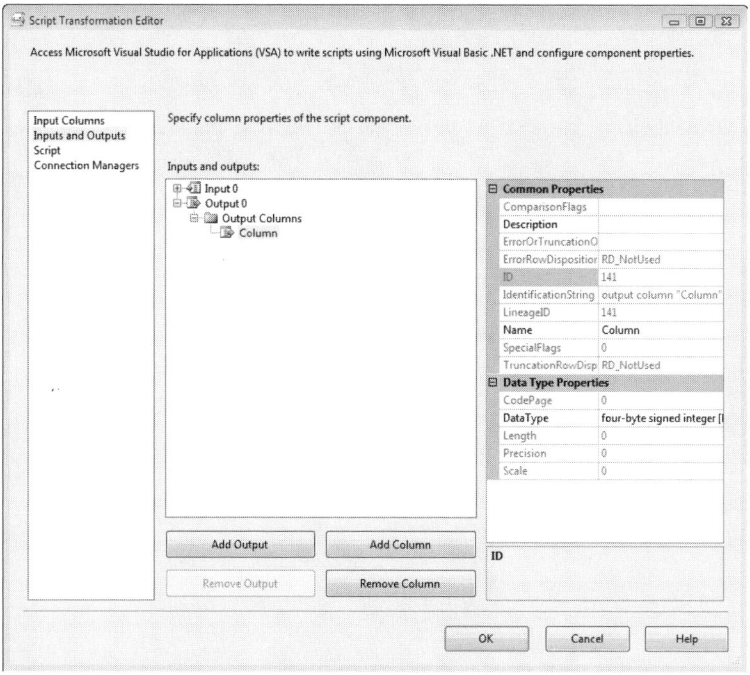

Figure 7.5: New Output Column.

This default column is not quite what we need. We can, however, edit its properties.

5. Edit the **Name** property of the column to be Soundex. The column name should change in the tree view, too.

6. SOUNDEX codes are strings, so select the **Data Type** property of the column and use the drop-down list to select the type **String [DT_STR]**.

Tech Tip:

[DT_STR] is an SSIS data type. SSIS data types are often slightly different from SQL, Visual Basic, or .NET Framework types. This is because SSIS uses very deterministic types in order to optimize memory usage. SQL and Visual Basic types can be less precise than SSIS types.

At this stage, your component should look Figure 7.6.

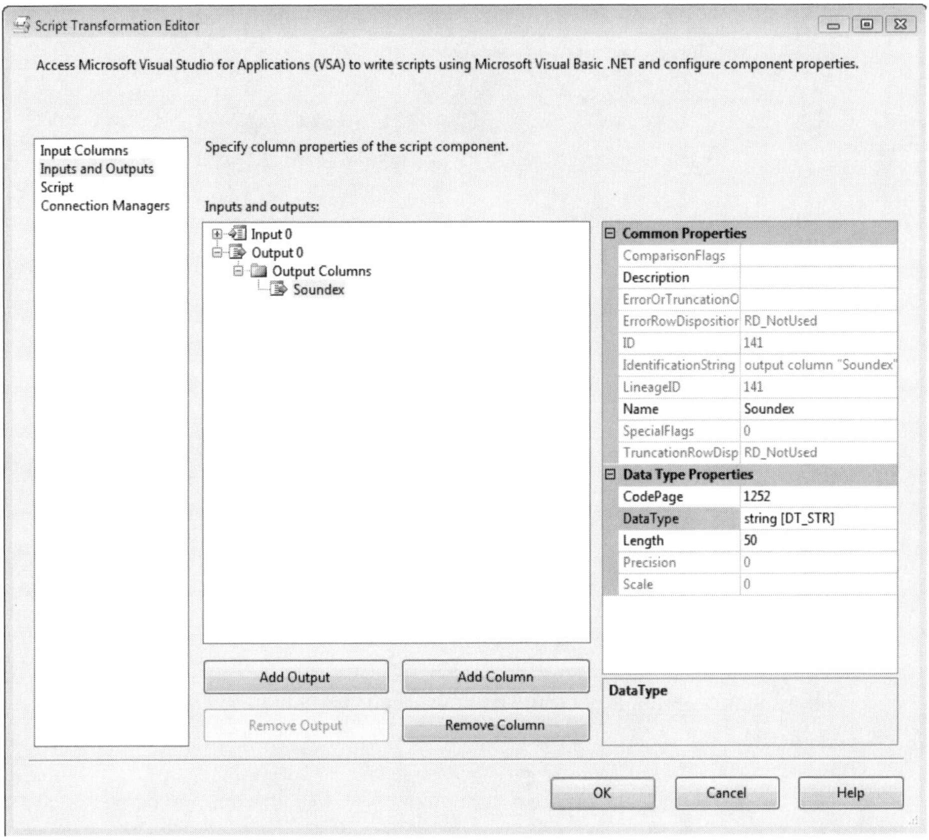

Figure 7.6: Renamed Output Column.

We have selected an Input Column (**LastName**) and created an Output Column (**Soundex**) to hold the transformed value. Now we are ready to write some code!

Elements of the Script

Navigate to the **Script** tab of the component. The component editor will now look like Figure 7.7.

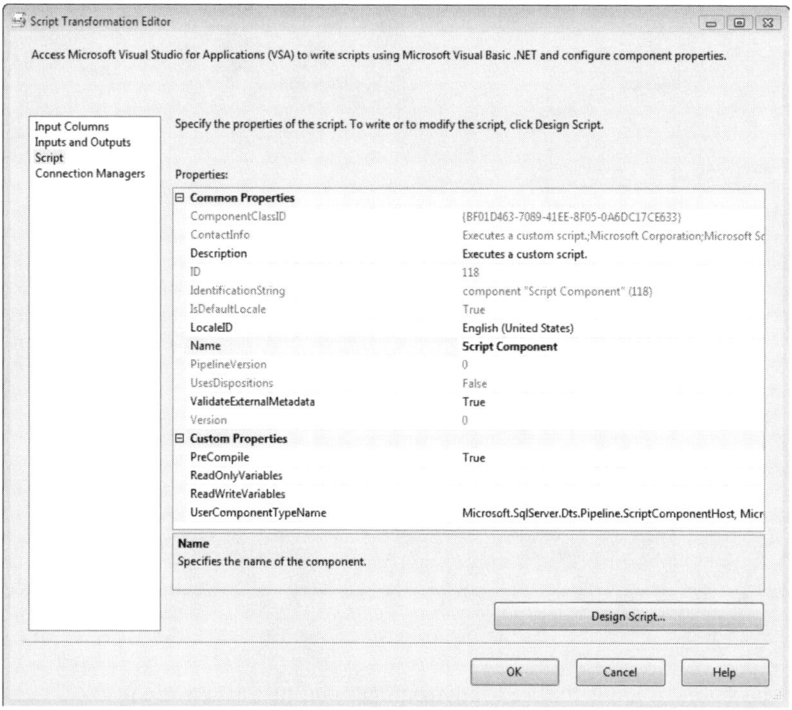

Figure 7.7: Script Tab of the Script Component.

There are some useful properties available in the property grid, but they are, in fact, optional. Note that the **PreCompile** property is set by default to `True`.

To get started, just click the **Design Script** button. The VSA editor will open, looking like Figure 7.8.

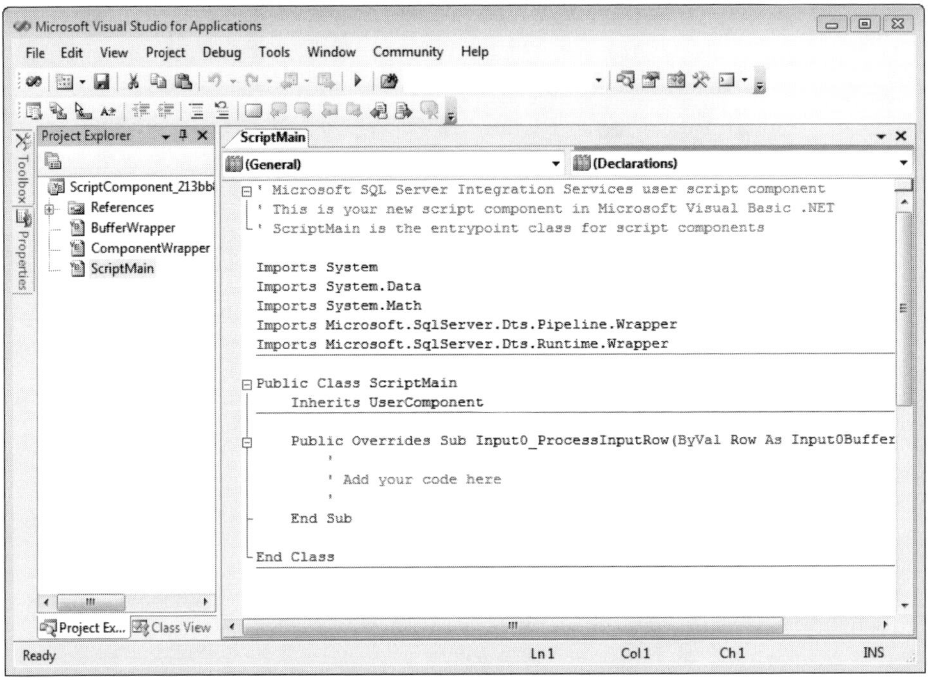

Figure 7.8: Script Editing Environment for a Component.

In Chapter 3, you learned about the VSA environment and its various elements. These should be familiar to you now, but some aspects of the script for a Script Component will certainly be new, compared to the Script Task we looked at earlier. First, look at the **Imports** statements for the Script Component in Listing 7.1.

```
Imports System
Imports System.Data
Imports System.Math
Imports Microsoft.SqlServer.Dts.Pipeline.Wrapper
Imports Microsoft.SqlServer.Dts.Runtime.Wrapper
```

Listing 7.1: Imports Statements for a Script Component.

You can see that rather than importing the `Dts.Runtime` namespace, there are two "wrappers" to be imported. These wrappers enable a script within a Data Flow Task to "see out" from the task to objects such as variables. In Chapter 8, you will learn that this introduces a slightly different way of accessing variables.

In the Script Task, the Main() subroutine was where most of the work was done, but here in the Script Component, we see something a little more involved, as in Listing 7.2.

```
Public Class ScriptMain
    Inherits UserComponent

    Public Overrides Sub Input_ProcessInputRow(ByVal Row As InputBuffer)
        '
        ' Add your code here
        '
    End Sub
End Class
```

Listing 7.2: ScriptMain Class in the Script Component.

The `ScriptMain` class performs those duties we mentioned earlier—wrapping and exposing the Data Flow columns and objects to the script. Within `ScriptMain` you can see the following subroutine: `Input0_ProcessInputRow(ByVal Row As InputBuffer)`. What does this mean? We will cover this in more detail later, but for now, all we need to know is that when the input to the Script Component is processed—specifically when the input named Input0 is processed—SSIS in effect calls this routine for every row. In practice, this means that we can immediately start writing useful script code.

Editing the Script Component

The example we are going to implement is a function to convert the customer's last name to a SOUNDEX code. Listing 7.3 shows the function that we will use for SOUNDEX, written in Visual Basic .NET code.

```
Function CalcSoundex(ByVal sName As String) As String
    Dim i, acode, dcode, prevCode As Integer
    Const codes As String = "01230120022455012623010202"
    SName = UCase(SName)
    CalcSoundex = Left(SName, 1)
    prevCode = Asc(Mid(codes, Asc(sName) - 64))

    For i = 2 To Len(SName)
        acode = Asc(Mid(SName, i, 1)) - 64
        ' we are not interested in symbols or numbers
        If acode >= 1 And acode <= 26 Then
            ' convert the character to a digit based on soundex code
            dcode = Asc(Mid(codes, acode, 1))
            ' ignore repeats
            If dcode <> 48 And dcode <> prevCode Then
                CalcSoundex = CalcSoundex & Chr(dcode)
                If Len(CalcSoundex) = 4 Then Exit For
            End If
            prevCode = dcode
        End If
    Next
End Function
```

Listing 7.3: A Simple SOUNDEX Function in VB.NET Script.

We do not really need to understand much about the internals of this function for this example. It returns a code based on the consonants in a string according to the SOUNDEX algorithm described earlier. For now, write this function into your script code, immediately after the `Input_ProcessInputRow` function, but still within `ScriptMain()`.

The next step is to reference the function in our script. For each row coming in to the component (in the input buffer) we will set the value of the **Soundex** column to the value returned by `CalcSoundex` based on the **LastName** column. Just below the line `Add your code here`, type: `Row`. That is, Row followed by a period. As shown in Figure 7.9, IntelliSense (within the editor) offers a list of options to complete this object, including the available columns (in this case **LastName** and **Soundex**).

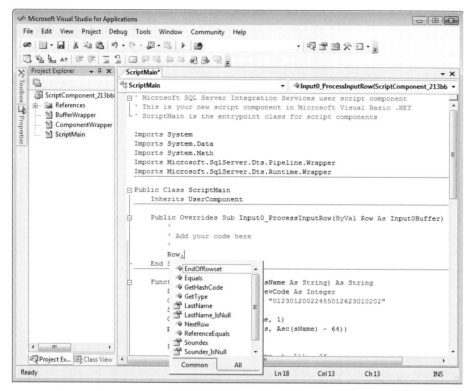

Figure 7.9: Using IntelliSense in the Scripting Environment.

In this case, select Soundex and complete the rest of the statement as shown in Listing 7.4, using IntelliSense if you like to complete the other references in this statement:

```
Row.Soundex = CalcSoundex(Row.LastName)
```

That is all! Your script is ready to run. Close the scripting environment. SSIS automatically saves the script for you. Now click the **OK** button in the Script Transformation Editor and return to the Data Flow design surface. The validation icon has now gone—your script is valid and you are ready to complete the Data Flow for testing.

Debugging the Script Component

In Chapter 5, you learned how to debug the Script Task by setting breakpoints within the script itself. The VSA design environment does enable you to set breakpoints in a Script Component, but the SSIS designer and debugger ignores them when executing a package.

There are a number of reasons for this, but it is mainly due to the nature of the Script Component , which (unlike the Script Task) does not call a script only once, but many times within an execution.

However, SSIS does provide some very elegant techniques for debugging Data Flows in general, and we can use these techniques to understand if our script is performing as expected. Later we will look at more fine-grained, row-by-row debugging. For now, we will see how to debug the script working against the Data Flow as many rows pass through it.

Debugging a Data Flow with a RowCount Component

You might think that you could execute the SSIS package right now, with just an OLE DB Source and a Script Component. In fact, this is possible, but not much will happen. If you were to try it, you would see no activity. You could find the explanation on the **Progress** tab of the designer, where you would see the following message:

```
Warning: Source "OLE DB Source Output" () will not be
read because none of its data ever becomes visible
outside the Data Flow Task.
```

SSIS has recognized that your data is not going anywhere, so it has optimized the Data Flow by removing the redundant components! Of course, the data from your Script Component (including your **Soundex** column) is not going anywhere, so you have no opportunity to see this data.

In most data-integration applications, you would send the data to a temporary destination in order to examine it and see if the process had transformed the data correctly. SSIS provides an excellent way to debug your data without having to create temporary tables or files.

The Row Count component simply counts the passing rows wherever you add it to the Data Flow. This component can be very useful for debugging. It gives you a count of the rows at a particular point and SSIS will not optimize it out of the Data Flow. This enables you to execute the Data Flow with a Row Count component at the end of the flow, even though you have added no destination. In other words, you can execute your SSIS package and debug it, even though the data is not going anywhere—it is just counting rows!

In Chapter 5, you learned how to create SQL Server Integration Services variables. Create a variable now, named *RowCount* of **Int32** type, as follows:

1. Select **SSIS⇨ Variables** to show the **Variables** window.

2. Click the **New Variable** button to create a new variable. This variable will be of type **Int32** by default.

3. Rename it to RowCount (see Figure 7.10). You can now close the **Variables** window if you like.

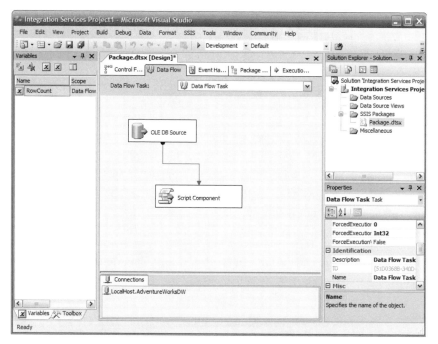

Figure 7.10: Data Flow Designer and Variables Window with RowCount Variable Added.

4. Drag a **Row Count Component** from the **Data Flow Transformations** tab of the **Toolbox** to the **Data Flow** design surface.

5. Now connect the output of the **Script Component** to the **Row Count Component**.

6. Edit the **Row Count** component by double-clicking the component shape in the designer.

7. In the **Advanced Editor for Row Count**, set the **VariableName** property to the name of the variable that you created: `RowCount`. With SP2 of SQL Server 2005, you will be able to select this variable from a dropdown list. Otherwise, you must enter the variable name manually.

If you were to execute the package now, the number of rows passing through the Row Count component would be written to the named variable.

Note:

The values of SSIS package variables used in a Data Flow do not change until the Data Flow has completed. This is true even when using the Script Component to write to a package variable.

Now that you can execute the package and the Data Flow within it, you can start to debug the output of the script. You shall see whether the script has calculated the SOUNDEX value correctly. The best way to see the output from the Script Component is to add a *data viewer* to the Data Flow on the path between the output of the Script Component and the input of the Row Count Component.

1. Right-click the line between path between the output of the **Script Component** and the input of the **Row Count Component**.

2. Select **Data Viewers**.

3. The **Data Flow Path Editor** will appear, with the **Data Viewers** tab visible by default (see Figure 7.11).

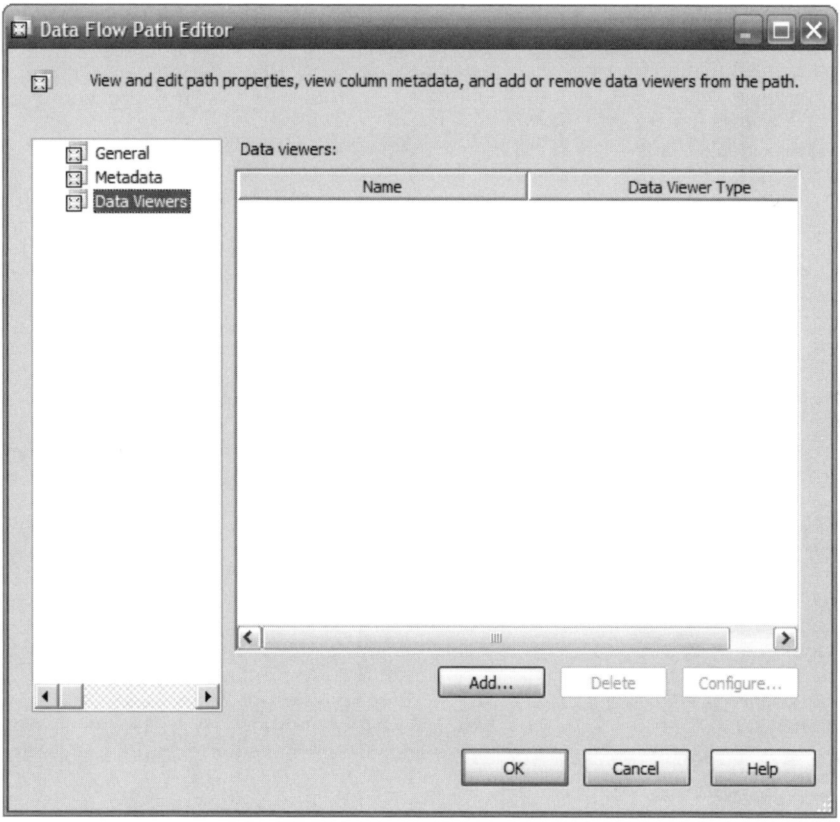

Data Flow Path Editor

View and edit path properties, view column metadata, and add or remove data viewers from the path.

General
Metadata
Data Viewers

Data viewers:

Name	Data Viewer Type

Add...   Delete   Configure...

OK   Cancel   Help

Figure 7.11: Data Flow Path Editor

4. Click the **Add ...** button in the **Data Flow Path Editor** to show the **Configure Data Viewer** dialog box (see Figure 7.12).

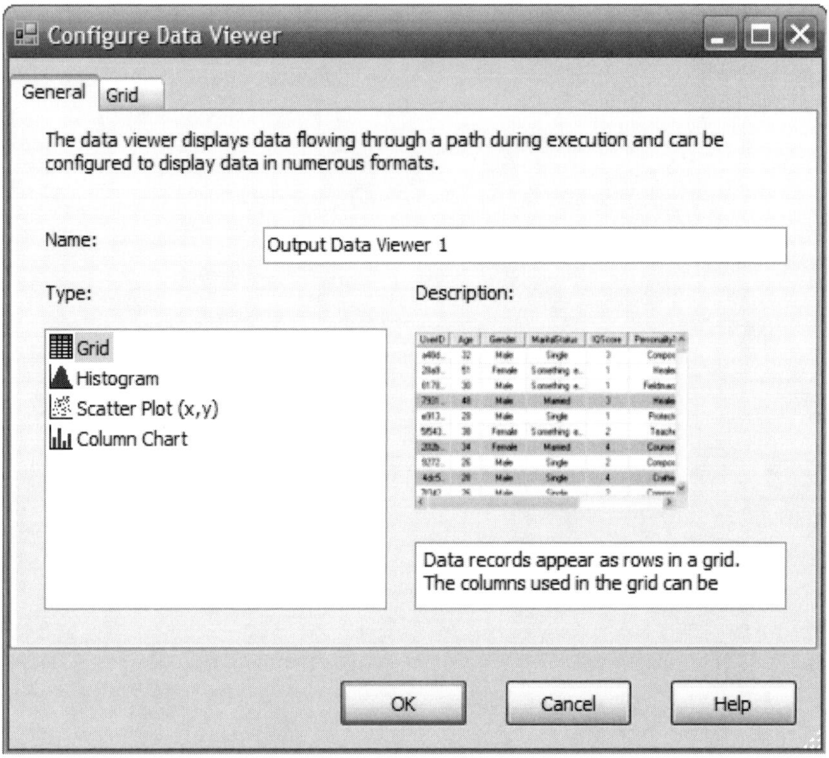

Figure 7.12: Configure Data Viewer Dialog Box.

5. Select the **Grid** type of Data Viewer, then click the **Grid** tab.

6. The **Grid** tab shows all the columns currently available selected on the right hand side. In fact, we only need to see the **LastName** and **Soundex** columns in order to debug our script. Use the arrow buttons to move all the other rows to the **Unused Columns** list on the left-hand side. In fact, it may be easier to move all the columns over to the left-hand side and reselect **LastName** and **Soundex** (see Figure 7.13).

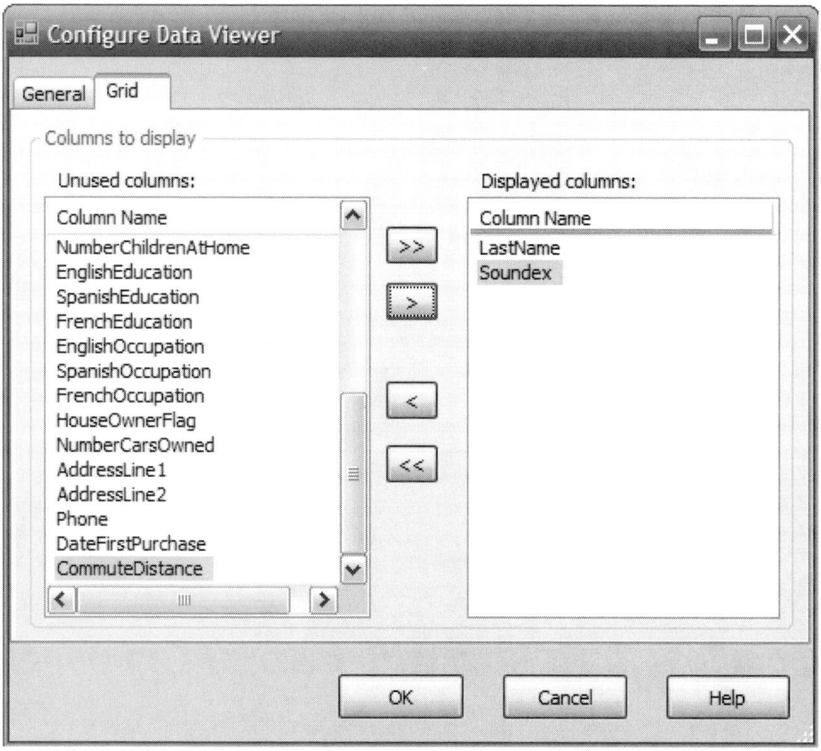

Configure Data Viewer

General | **Grid**

Columns to display

Unused columns:

Column Name
NumberChildrenAtHome
EnglishEducation
SpanishEducation
FrenchEducation
EnglishOccupation
SpanishOccupation
FrenchOccupation
HouseOwnerFlag
NumberCarsOwned
AddressLine1
AddressLine2
Phone
DateFirstPurchase
CommuteDistance

Displayed columns:

Column Name
LastName
Soundex

[>>] [>] [<] [<<]

[OK] [Cancel] [Help]

Figure 7.13: Grid Data Viewer Configured to Show Only Required Columns.

7.   Click the **OK** button to close the **Configure Data Viewer** dialog, and click
     OK again to close the **Data Flow Path Editor**.

Now the Data Flow is ready for debugging. The Data Flow designer shows the Data
Viewer on the path between the Script Component and the Row Count Component with a
"spectacles" icon (see Figure 7.14).

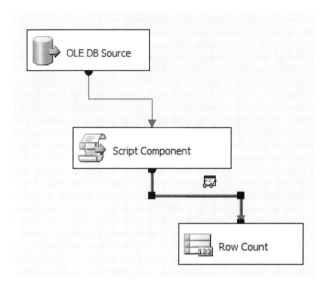

Figure 7.14: Completed Data Flow.

Running a Data Flow with a Script Component

To execute the package, and thus the Data Flow, you can use the **F5** key, or select **Debug⇨ Start Debugging** from the main menu, or right-click the package itself in the **Solution Explorer** and select **Execute Package**. When the package executes, you will notice that the **Data Viewer** window appears. You can drag and dock this Data Viewer to any size or convenient location in your designer or on your screen.

On execution, the Data Flow task reads a buffer of data from the OLE DB Source component. The Script Component acts on this buffer, transforming each row using our function. The Row Count component should next count these rows, but before it can do so, the Data Viewer will pause execution of the Data Flow and the package.

At this point, all the components in the flow will be colored yellow, to indicate that they are in progress and have not yet completed. When the Data Viewer has received a buffer of data, it displays the columns you selected in the viewer. As shown in Figure 7.15, the grid now shows the results of our SOUNDEX calculation for the first buffer of data—4872 rows.

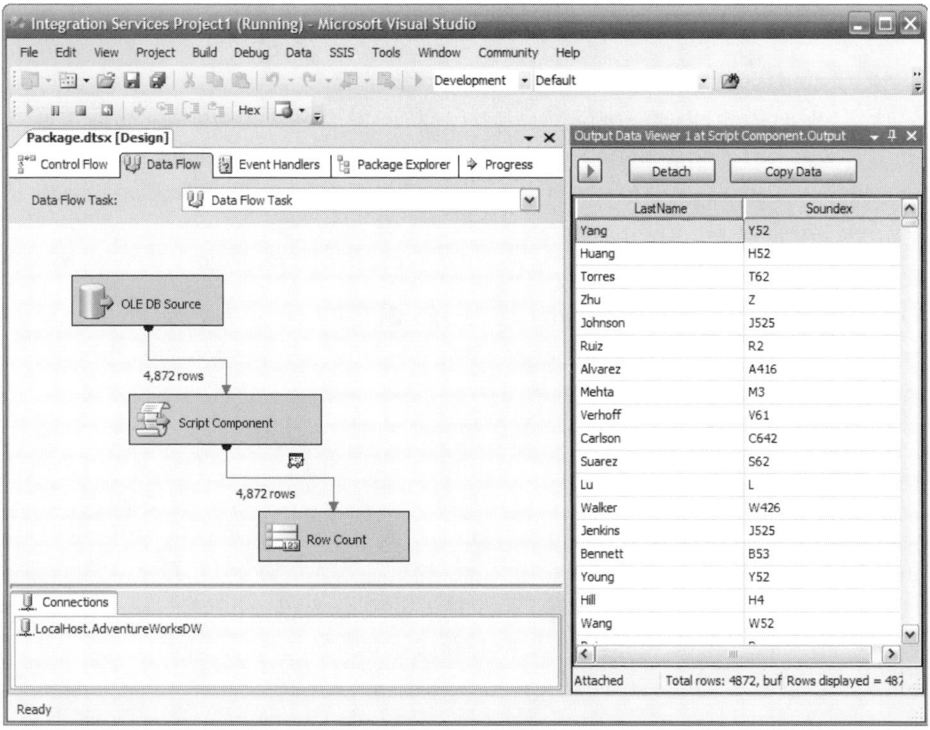

Figure 7.15: Data Flow Executed.

You can examine all the values to ensure that the function is working correctly. In this example they certainly appear to be correct. If necessary, you can even copy the data to the clipboard and paste it into other applications, such as Microsoft Excel, for further analysis.

To see the next buffer of data, click the green **Continue** button in the top left-hand corner of the Data Viewer. The Data Viewer will show the next buffer of data and pause again. Alternatively, if you have finished examining the data, you could click the **Detach** button and the flow will continue without pausing. Or, you could just close the Data Viewer.

Note:

If you detach the Data Viewer or close it, you will see the package execute without pausing. This will give you a good idea of the performance of the script component. You should find it to be excellent. Even on a Tablet PC, this script will calculate the SOUNDEX function for these 18484 rows in about 1-2 seconds!

When the Data Flow is complete, all the components in the Data Flow should be colored green to show that they have all completed successfully. You can now stop debugging, using **F5** if you like, just like any other SQL SSIS package.

Summary

As you can see, script components are versatile. They are easy to add to your Data Flow, quite simple to program, and give excellent performance. Add to that the power of visual debugging and you can see why they are such an exciting feature of SSIS. Mastering the Script Component can be your key to a vast range of data integration functionality.

Chapter 8

Asynchronous Script Components

In the last chapter, you learned how to add a script component to your Data Flow. One important step was adding an additional column to the output from the script component. Some components only change columns, or add columns to the output, but the output rows are still rows that pass through from the input. These are *synchronous* components—the output is synchronous with the input. This chapter shows how to create *asynchronous* components using script.

Asynchronous components have many uses. However, in all cases it is important to bear in mind that asynchronous components always create new output rows and that this requires some special handling.

An Asynchronous Top-n Rows Component

In this section, you will learn some more useful techniques for use with an asynchronous component. In particular, you will add rows to the output. You will also use a variable in your script component.

The component you will write is a top-*n* component. That is to say, that it will pass only the top-*n* rows from a sorted rowset to the output. This function is not available in SSIS, so you may find this script quite useful. In this scenario, we will sort by **CustomerAlternateKey**, and return the top *n* rows with the **CustomerAlternatekey**, **FirstName** and **LastName** columns. You will set the number of rows to select using a variable.

First, set up the package and the variable:

1. Create a new SSIS Package.

2. Select **SSIS** from the top-level menu.

3. Select **Variables** to show the **Variables** window.

4. Click the **New Variable** button to create a new variable.

5. This variable will be of type **Int32** by default. Rename it to `TopCount`.

6. Give this variable a useful default value. If you set this to 100, then by default the script will return the top 100 rows.

Next, set up the source adapter to deliver the rows:

1. Drag a **Data Flow Task** from the **Control Flow Items** tab of the **Toolbox** to the **Control Flow** design surface.

2. Double-click the **Data Flow Task** to open the **Data Flow** design surface.

3. Drag an **OLE DB Source** component from the **Data Flow Sources** tab of the Toolbox.

4. Double-click the **OLE DB Source** component shape on the design surface to open the **OLE DB Source Editor**.

5. Click the **New** button to create a new OLE **DB Connection Manager**.

6. Select an existing connection to your AdventureWorksDW database, or create a new one now.

7. Click the **OK** button to return to the **OLE DB Source Editor**.

8. Select the **Table or View Data Access Mode**.Select the `[dbo].[DimCustomer]` table.

9. Click the **OK** button to close the **OLE DB Source Editor**.

The top-*n* script requires a sorted input, so you should next add a Sort component. It would be possible to write a script that did not require a sorted input. For example, the script could manage an internal array of *n* rows. However, using a Sort component is a useful example of a modular or "toolkit" approach to building SSIS packages. The SSIS toolbox contains a large number of atomic components which can be chained together to build complex processes. This design approach enables you to build complex processes without reinventing the wheel at each step.

Use the following procedure to add a Sort component:

1. In the Designer, drag a **Sort** from the **Data Flow Transformations** tab of the **Toolbox** to the **Data Flow** design surface.

2. Connect the output of the **OLE DB Source** to the **Sort** component.

3. Double-click the **Sort** component shape on the design surface to open the **Sort Transformation Editor**.

4. In the **Available Input Columns** list box, check the box to the left of **CustomerAlternateKey** column. Notice that details of the sort operations for this column are now available in the grid at the bottom of the dialog.

5. In this grid, change the **SortType** for this column to **Descending**. This will ensure that the highest value rows are the first rows issued at the output.

6. On the right-hand side of the **Available Input Columns** list box, you will notice an option to **Pass Through** columns that are not sort keys. SSIS selects all columns by default. **Pass Through** simply means that the **Sort** component will add these columns to the output. **Sort** is an asynchronous component, and later you will see that you will explicitly add columns to the output of your asynchronous components, too.

7. You will only be using the **FirstName** and **LastName** columns, so you can uncheck all the others. It is good practice to pass through only columns that you will use later.

8. Click the **OK** button to close the dialog. The **Sort** component will sort your rows in ascending order, by the **CustomerAlternateKey** column.

> *Tech Tip:*
> The Sort component includes an option to "Remove rows with duplicate sort values." This is useful for de-duplicating data. Users often wonder where to find this functionality and look for an explicit de-duplication component. Now you know – it is tucked away within Sort! However, for more advanced de-duplication, SSIS also has the Fuzzy Grouping component that can find even approximate duplicates within data sets. It also returns a score of the similarity of the matches. Together, these capabilities enable some powerful data cleansing scenarios with SSIS.

Now that you have a sorted rowset, you can add the **Script** component:

1. In the Designer, drag a **Script Component** from the **Data Flow Transformations** tab of the **Toolbox** to the **Data Flow** design surface.

2. In the **Select Component Type** dialog box, select **Transformation**, and click the **OK** button.

3. Connect the output of the **Sort** to the **Script Component**.

4. Double-click the **Script Component** shape on the design surface to open the **Script Transformation Editor**.

5. On the **Input Columns** tab, check the box to select the **CustomerAlternateKey** column. You can leave the **Usage Type** of the column as **Read Only**. An asynchronous component writes its own output rows anyway, so these columns will not affected by anything you do in the script.

6. Check to select **FirstName** and **LastName** in the same way.

The next steps are to add your script, select the columns to work with, and add the output columns. Remember that the Sort component asked you which columns you wished to pass through, even though the Sort function did not act on them. In the same way, you will explicitly create all the output columns required by our component. In this case, we will just use `FirstName` and `LastName`.

1. Select the **Inputs and Outputs** tab of the **Script Transformation Editor**.

2. Select the **Output** node of the **Inputs and Outputs** tree view.

3. Edit the **Name** property of the output to be `MaxKeyOutput`.

4. Change the value of the output's **SynchronousInputID** property to `0`. This ensures you are writing an asynchronous component.

5. Expand the **Output** node of the **Inputs and Outputs** tree view.

6. Select the **Output Columns** folder under the **Output** node.

7. Click the **Add Column** button.

8. Edit the **Name** property of the column to be `CustomerAlternateKey`.

9. Select the **Data Type** property of the column and use the drop-down list to select the type **String [DT_STR]**. Set the length to 15. This column was a 15-character string at the input.

10. Click the **Add Column** button.

11. Edit the **Name** property of the column to be FirstName.

12. Select the **Data Type** property of the column and use the drop-down list to select the type **String [DT_STR]**. Set the length to 50. This column was a 50-character string at the input.

13. Repeat Steps 10 to 12 to create the `LastName` output column.

Notice that in Step 3 you renamed the Output. This is a convenience, but very useful in an asynchronous component. In a synchronous component, you will most often write scripts that do not explicitly refer to the Output at all. In such cases, there is little need to give the Output a distinctive name. However, in an asynchronous component, where you must reference the Output, it is much easier to refer to an Output with a useful name.

Now it is time to navigate to the **Script** tab of the component:

1. Add the name of your variable `TopCount` to the **ReadOnlyVariables** property.

2. Click the **Design Script** button to open the script-editing environment.

Notice that the default script now includes an additional subroutine, `CreateNewOutputRows`, shown in Listing 8.1.

```
' Microsoft Data Transformation Services user script component
' This is your new script component in Microsoft Visual Basic .NET
' ScriptMain is the entrypoint class for DTS Script Components

Imports System
Imports System.Data
Imports System.Math
Imports Microsoft.SqlServer.Dts.Pipeline.Wrapper
Imports Microsoft.SqlServer.Dts.Runtime.Wrapper

Public Class ScriptMain
    Inherits UserComponent

    Public Overrides Sub Input0_ProcessInputRow(ByVal Row As Input0Buffer)
        '
        ' Add your code here
        '
    End Sub

    Public Overrides Sub CreateNewOutputRows()
        '
        ' Add rows by calling AddRow method on member variable called
        ➲ "<Output Name>Buffer"
        ' E.g., MyOutputBuffer.AddRow() if your output was named "My Output"
        '
    End Sub

End Class
```

Listing 8.1: Default Script for an Asynchronous Component.

If you leave the `CreateNewOutputRows` subroutine in the script, SSIS calls it once, implicitly, when the script executes. You can call `CreateNewOutputRows` explicitly, too. However, this routine is most useful when you need to generate new rows that are very independent of anything at the input. You will make good use of this subroutine later, when writing a source component. For the top-n component, this subroutine is not used and you can delete it. Nevertheless, the CreateNewRows subroutine does contain some useful comments concerning how to add rows and how to reference outputs. You will learn more about these after you have created the script.

The full top-*n* script is as follows:

```
Imports System
Imports System.Data
Imports System.Math
Imports Microsoft.SqlServer.Dts.Pipeline.Wrapper
Imports Microsoft.SqlServer.Dts.Runtime.Wrapper


Public Class ScriptMain
    Inherits UserComponent
    Dim c As Integer = 0

    Public Overrides Sub Input0_Process
        InputRow(ByVal Row AsInput0Buffer)
        If c < CInt(Me.Variables.TopCount) Then
            MaxKeyOutputBuffer.AddRow()
            MaxKeyOutputBuffer.CustomerAlternateKey = Row.
            ➲ CustomerAlternateKey
            MaxKeyOutputBuffer.FirstName = Row.FirstName
            MaxKeyOutputBuffer.LastName = Row.LastName
            c += 1
        End If
    End Sub
End Class
```

Listing 8.2: Script to Return the Top-n Rows.

There are a number of interesting features here, including some important differences from both Script Tasks and synchronous Script Components.

First, as you learned in Chapter 7, there are two wrappers to be imported. Next, there is the **ScriptMain** class. There is a variable, c, declared in the **ScriptMain** class. Why declare a variable here, rather than in a subroutine? The reason is that SSIS calls the subroutine for each row. If you declared c in the subroutine, there would be a new instance of the variable for each row, resetting the value to the default each time. In this case, you are using the variable to count the number of rows until we reach your selected number, so you must declare it outside the subroutine.

The subroutine itself is quite simple. The first line simply checks to see if the count of rows, *c*, has reached the value of your `TopCount` variable. To perform the comparison, you must cast the value of the variable explicitly to a `CInt`. You must also refer to the variable somewhat differently when using wrappers in the Script Component.

In a Script Task, you would refer to a variable in this manner:

```
Dts.Variables("TopCount").Value
```

In a Script Component, you refer to the same variable as follows:

```
Me.Variables.TopCount
```

You may wonder if there is a more efficient way to do this. After all, in this script, the code asks for the value of the variable *every* time a row is processed, but the value will always be the same. Perhaps it would be better to read the variable once and then use that value for each row. Perhaps, then, the script could read the variable value when the class is initialized, in the same way as it sets the variable c to a value at that time?

In fact, that is not quite possible. The collection of variables is not available at that time. However, in Chapter 9 you will learn about some subroutines that enable this. For our purposes just now, the script can be slightly inefficient.

The next line of the script, `MaxKeyOutputBuffer.AddRow()`, is where you explicitly add a row to the output buffer, as you must do in an asycnhronous component. If you forget this line and attempt to write to the output, the script will fail. Note the naming convention used for this call:

```
<Output Name>Buffer.AddRow()
```

Because you named your output **MaxKeyOutput**, this call should be:

```
MaxKeyOutputBuffer.AddRow()
```

The lines shown in Listing 8.3 simply set the columns of the output row to the equivalent values for the current input row. In this case, the output columns have the same names as the input columns, but this need not be true in all cases. Finally, the count of rows is incremented. Note that after your top-*n* rows have been written to the Output buffer, the incoming rows still trigger `Input_ProcessInputRow`, but the script does not write them to the output.

```
MaxKeyOutputBuffer.AddRow()
MaxKeyOutputBuffer.CustomerAlternateKey = Row.CustomerAlternateKey
MaxKeyOutputBuffer.FirstName = Row.FirstName
MaxKeyOutputBuffer.LastName = Row.LastName
c += 1
```

Listing 8.3: Adding a Row to the Output of an Asynchronous Component.

To debug this script component, use the techniques that you learned in Chapter 7. Add a Row Count component and a Data Viewer to the Data Flow. See if the results are as you expect when you execute the package. The results of a typical run are shown in Figure 8.1.

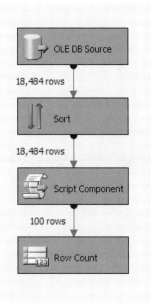

Figure 8.1: Debugging the Top-n Component.

> ### *Note:*
>
> If you are familiar with SSIS configurations, you will know you could *configure* the *TopCount* variable in this sample. A configuration enables you to change the value of the variable without editing the package, by supplying the new value in an XML file, for example. There is more information on configurations in the SSIS documentation.

Debugging a Script Component with Events

You will remember from Chapter 7 that Script Components cannot have breakpoints set within the script (unlike a Script Task). Nevertheless, there will be times when you need to examine values at a specific point in the script. Perhaps the easiest way to do this is to add a call to open a message box that will show the values of certain objects when the script reaches that line. For example, you could edit the top-n script as in Listing 8.4.

```
Public Class ScriptMain
    Inherits UserComponent
    Dim    c As Integer = 0

    Public Overrides Sub Input0_ProcessInputRow(ByVal Row As Input0Buffer)
        If c < CInt(ReadOnlyVariables.("TopCount").Value) Then
            MsgBox(c, MsgBoxStyle.Information, "Current    Row")
            MaxKeyOutputBuffer.AddRow()
            MaxKeyOutputBuffer.CustomerAlternateKey    = Row
            ➔ .CustomerAlternateKey
            MaxKeyOutputBuffer.FirstName = Row.FirstName
            MaxKeyOutputBuffer.LastName    = Row.LastName
            c += 1
        End If
    End    Sub
End    Class
```

Listing 8.4: Adding a Message Box to Debug a Script Component.

Here, a message box will appear for each of your top-*n* rows. This is reasonable at design time, but the message box is modal and it will halt the data flow until you manually close it. This is obviously not suitable for production packages that must run unattended.

For production, or to debug many rows, it is easier to fire an event from within your script. This is similar to firing an event from within a script task (see Chapter 6). Replace the line to call the message box with the code in Listing 8.5 to add an event to your Script Component.

```
Me.ComponentMetaData.FireInformation(1, "Top N Script", _
"Row " + (c + 1).ToString + " of " + _
Me.Variables.TopCount.ToString + " read", _
"", 0, True)
```

Listing 8.5: Adding an Event to Debug a Script Component.

Again, because you are accessing this object through the wrapper, the reference is somewhat different from when you used the Script Task.

Just like an event from the Script Task, you can also set up logging to write the details of this event to an SSIS log. However, if you just want to use it for debugging, you can simply execute the package. The **Progress** or **Execution Results** tabs will show the events too.

A Full-Rowset Asynchronous Component

The top-*n* component relied on a sorted input to identify the top values. It simply counted the top-*n* sorted rows then ignored the rest. In this way, the component gave a result based on the full rowset, but it did not need to evaluate the full rowset itself.

However, there may be times when it is not possible or desirable to prepare the data in this way before your script. For example, you may need to work with some attribute of the data, such as the length of strings that SSIS cannot prepare for you with standard components. Alternatively, you may not wish to incur the extra processing cost of sorting the data.

In such cases, you can script a full-rowset component where you process every row. In particular, you will need to handle the end of the incoming rowset explicitly. It is at that point that you will want to set the final values to be output.

In the next example, we will look at such a full-rowset component. The incoming data includes some product keys in the form of strings. The component will return the maximum product key, based on string comparisons, and the length of the longest string. As you may realize, the SSIS Aggregate component does not handle the maximum value of a string. It would be possible to calculate the longest string, but that would require some fancy footwork—using the expression language to calculate the length of each string row-by-row into a new derived column, and an aggregate to find the maximum value in that derived column.

Set up this example by following these steps:

1. Create a new SSIS Package.

2. Drag a **Data Flow Task** from the **Control Flow Items** tab of the **Toolbox** to the **Control Flow** design surface.

3. Double-click the **Data Flow Task** to open the **Data Flow** design surface.

4. Drag an **OLE DB Source** component from the **Data Flow Sources** tab of the **Toolbox**.

5. Double-click the **OLE DB Source** component shape on the design surface to open the **OLE DB Source Editor**.

6. Click the **New** button to create a new **OLE DB Connection Manager**.

7. Select an existing connection to your AdventureWorksDW database, or create a new one now.

8. Click the **OK** button to return to the **OLE DB Source Editor**.

9. Select the `Table or View` **Data Access Mode**.

10. Select the `[dbo].[DimProduct]` table.

11. Click the **OK** button to close the **OLE DB Source Editor**.

If you like, you can preview the data in the OLE DB Source Editor to see what is involved. You will be specifically interested in the **ProductAlternateKey** that contains widely varying values such as "BC-M005" or "FR-M21S-42."

Now that you have your data source, you can add the Script Component by following these steps:

1. In the Designer, drag a **Script Component** from the **Data Flow Transformations** tab of the toolbox to the **Data Flow** design surface.

2. In the **Select Component Type Dialog**, select **Transformation**, and click the **OK** button.

3. Connect the output of the **Sort** to the **Script Component**.

4. Double-click the **Script Component** shape on the design surface to open the **Script Transformation Editor**.

5. On the **Input Columns** tab, check the box to select the **ProductAlternateKey** column. You can leave the **Usage Type** of the column as Read Only.

6. Select the **Inputs and Outputs** tab of the **Script Transformation Editor**.

7. Select the **Output 0** node of the **Inputs and Outputs** tree view.

8. Edit the **Name** property of the output to be AggregateOutput.

9. Change the value of the output's **SynchronousInputID** property to None. This ensures you are writing an asynchronous component.

10. Expand the **AggregateOutput** node of the **Inputs and Outputs** tree view.

11. Select the **Output Columns** folder under the **Output** node.

12. Click the **Add Column** button.

13. Edit the **Name** property of the column to be MaxKey.

14. Select the **Data Type** property of the column and use the drop-down list to select the type **String [DT_STR]**. You can leave the length as a fifty-character string.

15. Click the **Add Column** button.

16. Edit the **Name** property of the column to be `LongestKey`.

17. Select the **Data Type** property of the column and use the drop-down list to select the type **String [DT_STR]**. You can leave the length as a fifty-character string.

Now it is time to navigate to the **Script** tab of the component. Click the **Design Script** button to open the script editor. The default script should be the same as for your previous asynchronous component. You can see the script for the full-rowset asynchronous component in Listing 8.6.

```
Imports System
Imports System.Data
Imports System.Math
Imports Microsoft.SqlServer.Dts.Pipeline.Wrapper
Imports Microsoft.SqlServer.Dts.Runtime.Wrapper


Public Class ScriptMain
    Inherits UserComponent
    Dim sMax As String = ""
    Dim lMax As String = ""


    Public Overrides Sub Input_ProcessInputRow(ByVal Row As InputBuffer)
    End Sub


    Public Overrides Sub Input_ProcessInput(ByVal Buffer As InputBuffer)
        While Buffer.NextRow
            If Buffer.ProductAlternateKey > sMax Then
                sMax = Buffer.ProductAlternateKey
            End If

            If Buffer.ProductAlternateKey.Length > lMax.Length Then
                lMax = Buffer.ProductAlternateKey
            End If
        End While
```

```
        If Buffer.EndOfRowset Then
            AggregateOutputBuffer.AddRow()
            AggregateOutputBuffer.MaxKey = sMax
            AggregateOutputBuffer.LongestKey = lMax
            AggregateOutputBuffer.SetEndOfRowset()
        End If
    End Sub
End Class
```

Listing 8.6: A Full-Rowset Asynchronous Component.

This script has a number of features that you have not previously encountered, but first, two variables are declared to hold the maximum string value and the longest string.

Notice the `Input_ProcessInputRow` subroutine. It has no code within it, yet in previous examples, this is where you have written the majority of your script in this routine. In fact, you could delete this routine for this example, but we are showing it here simply to emphasize that it has no code within it.

Previously, all your script components worked row-by-row. However, the previous scripts did not need to handle the end of the rowset explicitly. In this case, you need to know when you have reached the last row, in order to know when to write the aggregate values for the entire rowset to the output. To this end, the script uses the `Input_ProcessInput` subroutine. SSIS calls this subroutine once for every buffer of rows that arrives at the input. This can be thousands of rows at a time—SSIS will determine the buffer size. Therefore, when using this subroutine, you have to step through each row individually. You can see this in Listing 8.7. The code steps through each row in the buffer, comparing string values with the current maximum stored in the variables and updating when needed.

```
While Buffer.NextRow
    If Buffer.ProductAlternateKey > sMax Then
        sMax = Buffer.ProductAlternateKey
    End If
    If Buffer.ProductAlternateKey.Length > lMax.Length Then
        lMax = Buffer.ProductAlternateKey
    End If
End While
If Buffer.EndOfRowset Then
```

```
       AggregateOutputBuffer.AddRow()
       AggregateOutputBuffer.MaxKey = sMax
       AggregateOutputBuffer.LongestKey = lMax
       AggregateOutputBuffer.SetEndOfRowset()
End If
```

Listing 8.7: Stepping Through Rows in an Input Buffer.

After stepping through the rows, the script checks the incoming data to see if it has reached the end of the rowset. If so, it adds a new row to the output, and writes the current state of the variables to the relevant columns. The result is a one-row output.

The script also calls `SetEndOfRowset` explicitly to show that is has completed writing rows to the output buffer.

Lastly, note that this script does not use `CreateNewOutputRows`. When you first opened the script editor you would have noticed this subroutine, but you can delete it.

To debug this script component, add a Row Count component and a Data Viewer to the Data Flow as before. See if the results are as you expect when you execute the package. The results of a typical run are shown in Figure 8.2.

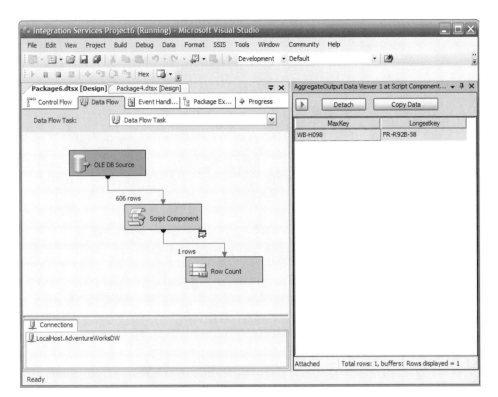

Figure 8.2: Debugging the String Aggregate Component.

Summary

In this chapter, you have learned how to write asynchronous components, explicitly adding outputs and writing rows to those outputs. In addition, you have seen you how to use variables and events in your script components. Through events, you can also log your script components. In the next chapter, we will look at some other interesting uses of Script Components—as sources and destinations in the Data Flow.

Did you know?

The VSA environment includes an Object Browser. Select the **View→Object Browser** menu item to open it. You can select assemblies which you reference in your script and browse them to find classes and methods that you can use.

Chapter 9

Script Sources
and Destinations

One of the trickiest situations that a data integration developer has to face is the client with files in a format that standard tools cannot parse. This is common in businesses with older legacy systems, but it can also occur in the most modern enterprises. Telephone services and Internet service providers frequently work with call detail records that log every call or every connection made. These records may come from many different makes and models of switch hardware, and each model may generate a different file format. Integrating all the call detail data into a warehouse can be a difficult task. Many companies have hundreds of lines of handcrafted code whose only purpose is to convert these files to more convenient formats in staging or transfer areas. From there, ETL tools or bulk loaders can read the more conventional format.

SSIS enables you to parse these non-standard files yourself, without having to land the data in a new format to a staging or transfer area. Moreover, having parsed the data using a script component, you can connect the output of that component just like any other, enabling you to build the most complex processing over your original data in a single process.

Developers may choose to write a custom source component to do this, and perhaps even distribute that component to other users of the same format. However, this chapter shows how to do this with a Script Data Source. The source that you will build can parse the format shown in Listing 9.1 and deliver it to an SSIS Data Flow.

```
RECORD_START
REC_ID:17804-4
BATCH_ID:02_2004_5
CUST_LNAME:MACLEOD
RECORD_END

RECORD_START
REC_ID:17815-2
ALT_REC_ID:Temp2_31
BATCH_ID:H1_2004_2
CUST_LNAME:MACLEAN
RECORD_END

RECORD_START
REC_ID:17222-1
BATCH_ID:01_2004_2
CUST_LNAME:MCLENNAN
RECORD_END
```

Listing 9.1: Non-Standard Text File Format for Parsing.

For this sample, you can create this file and save it as c:\customFile.txt. However, if you register this book at www.rationalpress.com, you can download a larger sample file.

In Listing 9.1, the text file data is arranged in rows with labels, rather than the column format that the SSIS Flat File Connection Manager expects. Each record spans several lines. The first line indicates the start of the record, and the last line indicates that the record is complete. Within each record, the information is irregular information. For example, the second record contains an ALT_REC_ID item that is not in the first. To load this to a database, it would be best to flatten this structure and deliver each record as a row, even though in some cases columns would be empty if a line was missing from that record.

A Script Source Component

You likely have a good idea how to add a script component already, as the **Select Script Component Type** dialog box appears whenever you add a script component. However, before you add the script, you should use the following steps to add a connection manager to make access to the file somewhat easier.

1. Create a new SSIS Package.

2. Right-click in the **Connection Managers** area at the foot of the SSIS Designer.

3. Select **Add New File Connection**. The **File Connection Manager Editor** will appear.

4. You will use an **Existing File**. Use the **Browse** button to select `c:\` `CustomFile.txt` where you saved the sample.

5. Click the **OK** button to close the **File Connection Manager Editor**. A new Connection Manager named **CustomFile.txt** will appear in the **Connection Managers** area.

Note that the connection manager you have added is for a File connection, not for a Flat File connection. The difference is important. A Flat File Connection Manager enables you to connect to a standard text data file, such as a comma- or tab- separated format. However, in addition to connection information, the Flat File Connection Manager also stores metadata describing the file, including column formats. A File connection simply enables you to connect to a file of any format—the metadata is your responsibility!

Now, add the Script component:

1. Drag a **Data Flow Task** from the **Control Flow Items** tab of the **Toolbox** to the **Control Flow** design surface.

2. Double-click the **Data Flow Task** to open the **Data Flow** design surface.

3. In the Designer, drag a **Script Component** from the **Data Flow Transformations** tab of the toolbox to the **Data Flow** design surface.

4. When you drag the **Script Component**, the **Select Component Type** dialog box will appear, prompting you to select the kind of component you want to create. You can see this dialog in Figure 7.2.

5. In the **Select Component Type** dialog box, select **Source** and click **OK**.

6. Double-click the **Script Component** shape on the design surface to open the **Script Transformation Editor**.

Do you notice anything different about the Script Transformation Editor at this point? There is no **Input Columns** tab. That should not be a surprise—a source has no inputs, only an output. In fact, you will notice that the default view is the **Inputs and Outputs** tab, but no inputs are available—only an output.

Select the default Output and rename it, if you like, to something more useful, such as RecordOutput. Note that the **SynchronousInputID** property is already 0. There is no input with which to synchronize.

In Chapters 7 and 8, you learned how to add columns to an Output. In this case, we need to add a column for every possible field in a record. Each column can be of string type. It is a good practice to keep your columns as short as possible, as this helps performance. SSIS can load more rows into memory if the columns are smaller. In this case, every column can be a 10-character string.

Add the following columns:

► REC_ID

► BATCH_ID

► CUST_LNAME

► ALT_REC_ID

Another feature of the Script Transformation Editor for sources is the **Connection Managers** tab. Use this tab to add references to connection managers you will be using in the script, according to the following steps:

1. On the **Connection Managers** tab, click **Add** to create a reference to a connection manager.

2. By default, this new reference will named **Connection**. You will use this name in your script, so it is good practice to rename it to something useful for you. In this case, rename it to `CustomFileConnection`.

3. In the **Connection Manager** column, select **customfile.txt** from the drop-down list. Note that you do have the option to create a new connection here, if you prefer.

Features of the Script for Sources

At this point, you have defined your output columns and referenced your connection manager. Now you can navigate to the **Script** tab, click the **Design Script** button, and view the default script in the editor. You can see the default script in Listing 9.2.

```
Imports System
Imports System.Data
Imports System.Math
Imports Microsoft.SqlServer.Dts.Pipeline.Wrapper
Imports Microsoft.SqlServer.Dts.Runtime.Wrapper


Public Class ScriptMain
    Inherits UserComponent

    Public Overrides Sub CreateNewOutputRows()
        '
        ' Add rows by calling AddRow method on member variable called
      ➲  "<Output Name>Buffer"
        ' E.g., MyOutputBuffer.AddRow() if your output was named "My Output"
        '
    End Sub
End Class
```

Listing 9.2: Default Script for a Source Component.

Again, there are differences between the default script for a source and the default script for a script transformation. The most significant difference is that there is no code for processing input rows. The only subroutine is `CreateNewOutputRows`. By now, you will not be surprised at that. There are no inputs, and a source only creates new rows.

As a first step to creating the script data source, you should make the changes shown in Listing 9.3.

```
Imports System
Imports System.Data
Imports System.Math
Imports Microsoft.SqlServer.Dts.Pipeline.Wrapper
Imports Microsoft.SqlServer.Dts.Runtime.Wrapper
Imports System.IO

Public Class ScriptMain
    Inherits UserComponent

    Public Overrides Sub CreateNewOutputRows()
        Dim oFile As File
        Dim oRead As StreamReader
        Dim LineIn As String

        Try
            oRead = oFile.OpenText(Me.Connections.CustomFileConnection
            ➲ .ConnectionString)

            While oRead.Peek <> -1
                LineIn = oRead.ReadLine()
                Me.ComponentMetaData.FireInformation(1, "script source", _
                LineIn, "", 0, True)
            End While
            RecordOutputBuffer.SetEndOfRowset()
        Catch e As Exception
            Me.ComponentMetaData.FireError(2, "script source", _
            e.Message, "", 0, True)
        Finally
            oRead.Close()
        End Try
    End Sub
End Class
```

Listing 9.3: Script Source Component to Read from a Text File.

The code is straightforward. It simply connects to the file and reads lines from it, sending each line to an OnInformation event. It is useful to note two details about this script. First, at this stage in development, the script only parses the file. It does not yet write output rows. So, if you connect this in the Data Flow and run the package, you will not see any data being output. Second, note the name of the output buffer—`RecordOutputBuffer`. This is what we renamed the output buffer. If you did not rename the output buffer, you would need to use the original name in the script too.

Now, let's look at some of the interesting details.

The following line imports a .NET Framework namespace that is convenient for using file readers and writers:

```
Imports System.IO
```

The script declares three variables:

```
Dim oFile As File
Dim oRead As StreamReader
Dim LineIn As String
```

`oFile` and `oRead` enable you to open the text file and read lines from it. `LineIn` will hold each line as you read it.

Notice the Try … Catch … Finally … EndTry block in Listing 9.3. This ensures that resources used by the script are properly closed. It is good practice to use this construct to protect resources in your code. See the Visual Basic .NET documentation for more details. When writing a script component, it is useful for debugging to fire an error event in the Catch block, as shown in this sample. In this way, you can recover important error information.

Using a Connection in Your Source Script

When the script runs, SSIS will acquire a connection to the file from the Connection Manager that you referenced in the Script Component Editor. It is good practice to use Connection Managers where you can in SSIS. They enable you to build more robust and flexible packages. In this case, using a Connection Manager would enable you to configure the connection string that points to your file. In this way, you could point to a file in a different location when in production without requiring an administrator to edit the package.

Listing 9.3 includes the following line to read in the connection sting for use by the StreamReader:

```
oRead = oFile.OpenText(Me.Connections.CustomFileConnection.
➲ ConnectionString)
```

The OpenText call is the standard way to open text files for reading with the .NET Framework classes. The usual parameter for this is simply the fully qualified name of the text file.

For our purposes, the parameter passed to it is more interesting, although ultimately it does still represent the fully qualified name of a text file. This parameter again uses the Me object to refer to the script component itself (which we saw previously Chapter 8). The Connections collection includes the connection manager you added in the Script Transformation Editor. You refer to it using the name you gave: CustomFileConnection. The **ConnectionString** property of a File Connection Manager is the path and name of the file, so we can pass this to the **OpenText** function:

```
While oRead.Peek <> -1
    LineIn = oRead.ReadLine()
    Me.ComponentMetaData.FireInformation(1, "script source", _
    LineIn, "", 0, True)
End While
```

In the While block, the script reads in the data from the file. The **Peek** method looks ahead one character at a time. If it reaches the end of the text file, it returns -1. Until the script reaches the end of the file, it reads in each line one at a time. At this stage, all we do is fire an Information event that will contain the newly read line. Later you will see that this helps us debug the script.

The lines `OutputBuffer.SetEndOfRowset()` and `oRead.Close()` perform some important housekeeping. One closes the file reader, and the other tells the output buffer to expect no more rows. You are now ready to debug the code so far.

In Chapter 8, you learned how to use **OnInformation** events to debug code. In fact, if you save this script, you can run this package right away—even though the Data Flow only contains a source. The package will not do much, but the information messages will be visible in the **Progress** and **Execution Results** tabs, and in the **Output** window, as shown in Listing 9.4.

```
Information: 0x1 at Data Flow Task, script source: RECORD_START
Information: 0x1 at Data Flow Task, script source: REC_ID:17804-4
Information: 0x1 at Data Flow Task, script source: BATCH_ID:02_2004_5
Information: 0x1 at Data Flow Task, script source: CUST_LNAME:MACLEOD
Information: 0x1 at Data Flow Task, script source: RECORD_END
Information: 0x1 at Data Flow Task, script source:
Information: 0x1 at Data Flow Task, script source: RECORD_START
Information: 0x1 at Data Flow Task, script source: REC_ID:17815-2
Information: 0x1 at Data Flow Task, script source: ALT_REC_ID:Temp2_31
Information: 0x1 at Data Flow Task, script source: BATCH_ID:H1_2004_2
Information: 0x1 at Data Flow Task, script source: CUST_LNAME:MACLEAN
Information: 0x1 at Data Flow Task, script source: RECORD_END
Information: 0x1 at Data Flow Task, script source:
Information: 0x1 at Data Flow Task, script source: RECORD_START
Information: 0x1 at Data Flow Task, script source: REC_ID:17222-1
Information: 0x1 at Data Flow Task, script source: BATCH_ID:01_2004_2
Information: 0x1 at Data Flow Task, script source: CUST_LNAME:MCLENNAN
Information: 0x1 at Data Flow Task, script source: RECORD_END
```

Listing 9.4: OnInformation Messages as the Script Source Reads a Text File.

Populating the Output

As you can see from Listing 9.4, the script appears to be reading the file correctly. If so, you can proceed to parse the column data from this format. The following version of **CreateNewOutputRows** in Listing 9.5 includes code to parse the data into columns. In addition, we have removed the **OnInformation** event now that we are satisfied with the code for reading the file.

```
Imports System
Imports System.Data
Imports System.Math
Imports Microsoft.SqlServer.Dts.Pipeline.Wrapper
Imports Microsoft.SqlServer.Dts.Runtime.WrapperImports System.IO


Public Overrides Sub CreateNewOutputRows()
    Dim oFile As File
    Dim oRead As StreamReader
    Dim LineIn As String

    Try
        oRead = oFile.OpenText(Me.Connections.CustomFileConnection.
        ➲ ConnectionString)

        While oRead.Peek <> -1
            LineIn = oRead.ReadLine()
            If LineIn.StartsWith("RECORD_START") Then
                RecordOutputBuffer.AddRow()
            ElseIf LineIn.StartsWith("REC_ID:") Then
                RecordOutputBuffer.RECID = LineIn.Remove(0, 7)
            ElseIf LineIn.StartsWith("ALT_REC_ID:") Then
                RecordOutputBuffer.ALTRECID = LineIn.Remove(0, 11)
            ElseIf LineIn.StartsWith("BATCH_ID:") Then
                RecordOutputBuffer.BATCHID = LineIn.Remove(0, 9)
            ElseIf LineIn.StartsWith("CUST_LNAME:") Then
                RecordOutputBuffer.CUSTLNAME = LineIn.Remove(0, 11)
            End If
        End While
        RecordOutputBuffer.SetEndOfRowset()
    Catch e As Exception
        Me.ComponentMetaData.FireError(1, "script source", e.Message, _
        "", 0, True)
    Finally
        oRead.Close()
```

```
    End Try
End Sub
```

Listing 9.5: CreateNewOutputRows Subroutine to Populate Source Component Output.

The code to generate the output rows is deliberately simple, but it does make the logic quite clear. The .NET Framework makes parsing the incoming text very easy. The simple call to AddRow and setting the output column values should be familiar to you from Chapter 8.

With this script in place, you should be able add a variable and Row Count Component, along with a Data Viewer as described in Chapter 7. With these, you can debug the script source. Once you are satisfied that the script source is working correctly, you could introduce more components to the data flow to perform subsequent transformations.

Using Multiple Outputs

Of course, it is possible to add many more features to this component. For example, what happens to lines that do not meet any of the criteria we have specified? Perhaps these lines are errors, or comments. In such cases, it would be convenient to be able to stream these exception rows to another output. From there, the package developer could direct them to a destination for later analysis.

It is quite easy to add multiple outputs to a Script Component in SSIS, but do note that you cannot have multiple inputs. Script Components only support one input. To add a second output to this component, follow these steps:

1. Double-click the **Script Component** shape on the design surface to open the **Script Transformation Editor**.

2. On the **Inputs and Outputs** tab, click **Add Output** to add a new output.

3. Select the new Output node (**Output 1**) of the **Inputs and Outputs** tree view.

4. Edit the **Name** property of the output to be BadRowOutput. The tree view will show the new name.

5. Again, the output's **SynchronousInputID** property is already None. There is no input with which to synchronize.

6. Expand the **BadRowOutput** node of the **Inputs and Outputs** tree view.

7. Select the **Output Columns** folder under the **Output** node.

8. Click the **Add Column** button.

9. Edit the **Name** property of the column to be `UnparsedRow`.

10. Select the **Data Type** property of the column and use the drop-down list to select the type **String [DT_STR]**. The default length of 50 should be enough for this case, but in many cases might need to be longer. Remember that this column will contain an entire row.

The version of **CreateNewOutputRows** in Listing 9.6 uses this new **BadRowOutput** to hold rows that did not parse into the predefined columns.

```
Public Overrides Sub CreateNewOutputRows()
    Dim oFile As File
    Dim oRead As StreamReader
    Dim LineIn As String

    Try
        oRead = oFile.OpenText(Me.Connections.CustomFileConnection.
        ➲ ConnectionString)
        While oRead.Peek <> -1
            LineIn = oRead.ReadLine()
            If LineIn.StartsWith("RECORD_START") Then
                RecordOutputBuffer.AddRow()
            ElseIf LineIn.StartsWith("REC_ID:") Then
                RecordOutputBuffer.RECID = LineIn.Remove(0, 7)
            ElseIf LineIn.StartsWith("ALT_REC_ID:") Then
                RecordOutputBuffer.ALTRECID = LineIn.Remove(0, 11)
            ElseIf LineIn.StartsWith("BATCH_ID:") Then
                RecordOutputBuffer.BATCHID = LineIn.Remove(0, 9)
            ElseIf LineIn.StartsWith("CUST_LNAME:") Then
                RecordOutputBuffer.CUSTLNAME = LineIn.Remove(0, 11)
            ElseIf Not (LineIn.StartsWith("RECORD_END") Or _
            LineIn = "") Then
```

```
                BadRowOutputBuffer.AddRow()
                BadRowOutputBuffer.UnparsedRow = LineIn
            End If
        End While
        BadRowOutputBuffer.SetEndOfRowset()
        RecordOutputBuffer.SetEndOfRowset()
    Catch e As Exception
        Me.ComponentMetaData.FireError(1, "script source", e.Message, _
        "", 0, True)
    Finally
        oRead.Close()
    End Try
End Sub
```

Listing 9.6: Directing Rows to a Second Output.

The following excerpt from Listing 9.6 shows the code that handles the lines which the previous logic does not catch:

```
ElseIf Not (LineIn.StartsWith("RECORD_END") Or _
LineIn = "") Then
    BadRowOutputBuffer.AddRow()
    BadRowOutputBuffer.UnparsedRow = LineIn
```

You should also call **SetEndOfRowset** for the new output. Note that we ignore **RECORD_END** and empty rows, as we expect some of these in our file format. If you have downloaded the sample file, then there are some bad rows included within it. If you have created the file yourself, you can add some bad rows.

To debug the data flow, simply add a second variable and Row Count Component. Connect an output from the Script Component to the Row Count Component. You have two outputs from the Script Component and one should already be in use. Therefore, the Designer will automatically select the **BadRowOutput** when connecting to the new Row Count. Now you can add a data viewer, and debug both outputs.

> ⚠️ **Caution:**
>
> To debug a multiple-output source, you can use multiple data viewers on different paths in a data flow. In such cases, be aware that Data Viewers work one at a time. The data for one path will be shown first in its viewer. Then, when you click the green arrow in the first viewer, the data on the next path will appear in the next data viewer. To continue, you can repeatedly toggle between the viewers in this way, or you can detach both viewers.

A Script Destination Component

Reading from custom or legacy file formats is a very common scenario. Writing back to those formats is less common, but still required in some businesses where the system developer must exchange data to and from custom applications. In addition, there are formats that SSIS does not natively support.

For example, SSIS does not include an XML destination. This may be surprising, because SSIS does include an XML source. However, sources and destinations have quite different requirements, especially for a hierarchical structure such as XML. It is straightforward for a source adapter to parse a single hierarchical document into multiple outputs—one per level of the hierarchy. In contrast, a destination adapter has to take multiple, possibly unrelated inputs, and from them compose a properly structured hierarchical output.

In this example, we will create a much simpler scenario, in which a script destination adapter creates a simple XML document from the custom source we completed earlier. In other words, you will use SSIS and scripting to convert data from a custom format to XML. The advantage of doing this in SSIS is that you can easily add debugging, logging, error handling to the conversion, while also using the Control Flow to integrate the conversion in a wider process. This should give a good impression of the power of scripting in SSIS.

Adding the Script Destination

Use the following procedure to add the script destination. You will use the SSIS package that you created in the previous custom source example.

1. Delete the **RowCount** component that you used to debug the **RecordOutput** from the source **Script Component**.

2. In the Designer, drag a **Script Component** from the **Data Flow Transformations** tab of the **Toolbox** to the **Data Flow** design surface.

3. When you drag the Script Component, the **Select Component Type** dialog box will appear, prompting you to select the kind of component you want to create.

4. Select **Destination** and click the **OK** button.

5. Connect an output from the source **Script Component** to the new **Script Component**. If you already connected the **BadRowOutput** to a component, then SSIS will select **RecordOutput** by default. Otherwise, be sure to select **RecordOutput** yourself.

6. Double-click the new **Script Component** shape on the design surface to open the **Script Transformation Editor**. You will notice that, unlike the script source, a script destination does have an **Input Columns** tab.

7. On the **Input Columns** tab, check the boxes to select all the incoming columns. You can leave the **Usage Type** of each column as ReadOnly because columns will not be affected by anything you do in the script. To select all columns quickly, you can use **Ctrl+A**, the **Shift+DownArrow**, or **Shift+UpArrow**.) Having selected all the columns, if you check the box for any one of them, you will check the boxes for all of them.

8. Select the **Inputs and Outputs** tab of the **Script Transformation Editor**.

9. Select the **Input 0** node of the **Inputs and Outputs** tree view.

10. Edit the **Name** property of the input to be something useful, such as ParsedInput.

11. On the **Connection Managers** tab, click **Add** to create a reference to a connection manager.

12. By default, this new reference will be named **Connection**. You will use this name in your script, so it is good practice to rename it to something useful for you. In this case, rename it to `XMLConnection`.

13. In the **Connection Manager** column, select <**New Connection...**> from the drop-down list.

14. The **File Connection Manager Editor** will appear.

15. Your destination will be creating a new file; therefore, you should select **Create File** from the drop-down list. Use the **Browse** button to select the **C:** folder and enter `XCustomer.xml` as the file name.

16. Click the **OK** button to close the **File Connection Manager Editor**. A new Connection Manager named **XCustomer.xml** will appear in the **Connection Managers** area.

17. Ensure that you have selected your new connection to **XCustomer.xml** in the **Connection Manager** column. You may need to select it again to ensure it appears in this column correctly.

Features of the Script for Destinations

At this point, you have defined your input columns and referenced your connection manager. Now you can navigate to the **Script** tab, click **Design Script**, and view the default script shown in Listing 9.7.

```
Imports System
Imports System.Data
Imports System.Math
Imports Microsoft.SqlServer.Dts.Pipeline.Wrapper
Imports Microsoft.SqlServer.Dts.Runtime.Wrapper

Public Class ScriptMain
    Inherits UserComponent
```

```
Public Overrides Sub ParsedInput_ProcessInputRow(ByVal Row As
➲  ParsedInputBuffer)
        '
        ' Add your code here
        '
    End Sub
End Class
```

Listing 9.7: Default Script for Destination Component.

There are differences here, too, between the default script for a destination and the default for a source. In fact, a destination is most similar to a synchronous transformation.

Remember that a synchronous component cannot add rows to the output, but it can remove them and transform them. On the other hand, an asynchronous component *must* add rows to an output itself. A source component, therefore, is a special asynchronous component with no inputs. In the same way, a destination component is a special synchronous transformation with no output. For this reason, in the default script for a destination shown in Listing 9.7, there is only code for processing input rows.

An XML Destination Component

The first step to creating an XML destination is to add a reference to the System.XML assembly. This is not just a question of using an **Imports** statement. You will have to add the System.XML assembly to your script project.

1. Select **Project**⇨ **Add Reference** from the main menu of the VSA script environment. The **Add Reference** dialog box will appear (see Figure 6.7 in Chapter 6).

2. Select the assembly named **System.XML.dll**.

3. Click the **Add** button. **System.XML.dll** should appear in the **Selected Projects and Components** list at the foot of the **Add Reference** dialog box.

4. Click the **OK** button to close the dialog box and return to the script.

A reference to the System.XML assembly now exists in your project and is ready for use. You can check this by selecting **View**⇨ **Project Explorer** from the main menu of the VSA script environment. The Project Explorer window will appear. Expand the References to see your project references.

Now you are ready to edit your script to create an XML destination component, as shown in Listing 9.8.

```
Imports System
Imports System.Data
Imports System.Math
Imports Microsoft.SqlServer.Dts.Pipeline.Wrapper
Imports Microsoft.SqlServer.Dts.Runtime.Wrapper
Imports System.Xml


Public Class ScriptMain
    Inherits UserComponent
    Dim xWriter As XmlTextWriter

    Public Overrides Sub PreExecute()
        xWriter = New XmlTextWriter _
            (Me.Connections.XMLConnection.ConnectionString, _
            Nothing)
        xWriter.WriteStartDocument()
        xWriter.WriteComment("Customer file parsed using script")
        xWriter.WriteStartElement("x", "customer", _
            "http://some.org/name")
        xWriter.WriteAttributeString("FileName", _
            Me.Connections.XMLConnection.ConnectionString)
    End Sub

    Public Overrides Sub ParsedInput_ProcessInputRow(ByVal Row As _
    ParsedInputBuffer)

        xWriter.WriteStartElement("CUSTOMER")

        xWriter.WriteStartElement("BATCH_ID")
        xWriter.WriteString(Row.BATCHID)
```

```
        xWriter.WriteEndElement()
        xWriter.WriteStartElement("RECID")

        xWriter.WriteString(Row.RECID)
        xWriter.WriteEndElement()
        xWriter.WriteStartElement("ALTRECID")

        xWriter.WriteString(Row.ALTRECID)
        xWriter.WriteEndElement()
        xWriter.WriteStartElement("CUSTLNAME")

        xWriter.WriteString(Row.CUSTLNAME)
        xWriter.WriteEndElement()
        xWriter.WriteEndElement()
    End Sub

    Public Overrides Sub PostExecute()
        xWriter.WriteEndElement()
        xWriter.WriteEndDocument()
        xWriter.Close()
    End Sub

End Class
```

Listing 9.8: XML Destination Script.

The first change to note is the line that imports the namespace for the System.Xml assembly:

```
Imports System.Xml
```

Next, notice that the script declares an **XmlTextWriter**. The script declares this within the class, but not within a subroutine:

```
Dim xWriter As XmlTextWriter
```

In this way, all subroutines can use the **XmlTextWriter**.

> ### Note:
> **XmlTextWriter is a .NET Framework class for creating XML documents. The class enables you to write well-formed XML easily. The XmlTextWriter class contains methods for starting and completing a document, along with methods for writing elements and attributes. More information on this class is available with the .NET Framework documentation.**

PreExecute and PostExecute

This script includes two new subroutines: `PreExecute` and `PostExecute`. As their names suggest, SSIS calls these subroutines before and after the execution of the component. They are very useful for performing operations that need only occur once, often to create and release objects that other subroutines will use during execution. In this case, `PreExecute` uses the `ConnectionString` of the connection manager to open an `XmlTextWriter` that will enable you to write well-formed XML to that file.

This routine also prepares the `XmlTextWriter` by calling `WriteStartDocument`. It immediately writes a comment (which is optional, of course).

> ### Note:
> **The `PreExecute` routine helps to solve the problem you encountered in Chapter 8. Remember that the script read a variable value for every row, even though the variable value would not change from row to row. You could add the following code to the ScriptMain class in Listing 8.2:**
> ```
> Dim tc As Integer = 0
> Public Overrides Sub PreExecute()
>     tc = CInt(Me.Variables.TopCount.Value)
> End Sub
> ```
> **This would cache the value of the variable at the beginning of package execution. Now you can replace the line:**
> ```
> If c < CInt(Me.Variables.TopCount.Value)
> ```
> **with ...**
> ```
> If c < tc
> ```
> **This is a much more efficient operation.**

When using the XmlTextWriter, you typically start and end an XML element. Note that this script starts writing the top-level element in PreExecute. During execution of the component, it writes more elements of the document. Finally, the script writes the end of the top-level element in PostExecute, which also writes the end of the document and closes the XmlTextWriter.

When this component executes, it calls the subroutine ParsedInput_ProcessInputRow for each row passing. Note that the default script bases the name of this routing on the name of the input. For each row, it first writes the start of an element, CUSTOMER, that will contain all the column values for the row. The script writes a separate string element for each column, before finally writing the end of the CUSTOMER element.

Once you have edited this script, you will be ready to debug the data flow. In this case, you do not need to add a variable and Row Count Component to debug. All you need to do is to execute the package and, when the package is finished, examine the XML file in your favorite XML editor, or Microsoft Internet Explorer. It is a good idea to close your XML editor while running the package, to ensure that it does not lock the XML file while SSIS is trying to write to it.

Summary

Many enterprises have data in formats that are unique to them, or that the integration designer cannot handle with standard interfaces through SSIS or other tools. These problems can be a real barrier to effective data integration. With scripting, SSIS enables users to quickly and easily write and debug their own data sources or data destinations. In this way, you can deliver many practical solutions to otherwise thorny situations.

The next chapter looks at some other practical solutions, to give you an idea of how effective SSIS scripting can be in solving data integration problems.

Did you know?

Experienced SQL Server users often ask me how fast SSIS is compared to DTS in SQL Server 2000. The short, but incomplete, answer is "Much faster."

DTS was actually very fast at simple data loading into SQL Server. In fact, the database largely determined performance. However, to transform data, DTS used ActiveX script, which was very slow. The speed of DTS often depended on the number and complexity of these scripts.

SSIS transforms data using powerful native components, which greatly outperform DTS. Even when extending packages with script, SSIS compiles the script and is very much faster than ActiveX.

Direct comparisons are difficult. You will design many patterns quite differently between DTS and SSIS. However, in tests designed to be as similar as possible, I often find SSIS to be at least seven times faster than DTS.

At the high end of performance, SSIS can be an order of magnitude faster, due to the power of the highly optimized data flow engine.

Applying Scripts in Practice

Chapter 10

Useful Examples

Now that you are becoming more expert with scripting, this chapter will concentrate less on systematic instructions. Instead, it will simply show examples of interesting scripts and explain the principles involved. In this way, you will quickly learn how to solve some common problems, while acquiring practice and a deeper understanding of SSIS scripting.

Regular Expressions

The first example uses the .NET Framework **Regex** class to bring the power of regular expressions to your SSIS components. The script will use a regular expression to validate e-mail addresses in a database. In addition, the script will extract the user name and e-mail host from the address to new columns. It will also add a Boolean flag to indicate whether the original address was valid or not.

Setting Up the Source and Script Component

By now, you should be familiar with the steps to add a script component and edit it. Therefore, we will keep the setup instructions to a minimum.

1. Create a new package.

2. Add an OLEDB Connection Manager for your AdventureWorksDW sample database.

3. Add a Data Flow Task.

4. Add an OLEDB Source component.

5.   Select the **DimCustomer** table from AdventureWorksDW.

6.   Add a Script Component.

7.   Select it to be a Transformation component.

8.   Connect the output of the OLEDB Source component to the Script Component. This Script Component will be synchronous—the script will calculate new columns for each row as it passes.

9.   On the **Input Columns** tab, select **EmailAddress**. Keep the **UsageType** as **ReadOnly**.

10. On the **Inputs and Outputs** tab, add three new output columns, as shown in Table 10.1:

Column Name	Column Type
MailHost	String [DT_STR]
UserName	String [DT_STR]
EmailValid	Boolean [DT_BOOL]

Table 10.1: Three New Output Columns.

There is no need to change the default lengths of these columns. Now you are ready to edit the script.

The Script

The script in Listing 10.1 is straightforward. Note that the script imports System.Text. RegularExpressions.

```
Imports System
Imports System.Data
Imports System.Math
Imports Microsoft.SqlServer.Dts.Pipeline.Wrapper
Imports Microsoft.SqlServer.Dts.Runtime.Wrapper
Imports System.Text.RegularExpressions


Public Class ScriptMain
    Inherits UserComponent
```

```
Dim EmailTest As Regex = New _ Regex("(?<username>[^@]+)@(?<mailhost>.+)")
Dim m As Match

Public Overrides Sub Input_ProcessInputRow(ByVal Row As _ InputBuffer)
    m = EmailTest.Match(Row.EmailAddress)
    If m.Success Then
        Row.MailHost = m.Groups("mailhost").Value
        Row.UserName = m.Groups("username").Value
        Row.EmailValid = True
    Else
        Row.EmailValid = False
    End If
End Sub
End Class
```

Listing 10.1: Script Component Using Regular Expressions.

Hook up the output of your script component to a RowCount component with a suitable variable for debugging. Figure 10.1 shows an example of the output from this component.

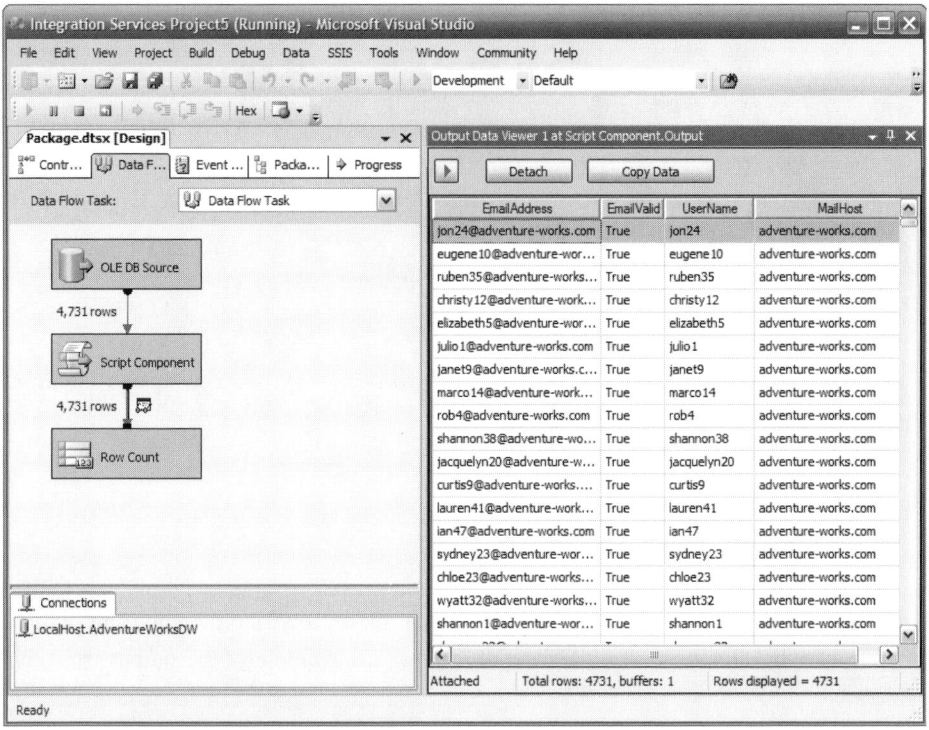

Figure 10.1: Debugging the Regular Expression Component.

FREE *Bonus:*

When running this sample with AdventureWorksDW, you will find that all its e-mail addresses are valid. You may find it useful either to edit the source data or to try this script with some other data source of your own. However, if you register this book at www.rationalpress. com, you can download a sample of this script, which includes a text file source that you can modify for debugging.

Calculating a Hash for Change Data Capture

Knowing when data has changed is important in many scenarios, especially for handling incremental loads from sources. Some source schemas have columns to help with this specifically, including the timestamp of the last change. However, many source systems do not have this information, and often, sources are in formats or in applications that even administrators cannot modify.

In such cases, it is useful to calculate a hash or checksum of the data. You can calculate the hash for all the columns in the source row and include it with the data when loading from the source to the destination. The next time you query the source, you can calculate the hash for the source data again. Now the SSIS process can lookup to the destination, find the matching row based on its key, and compare the hash values. If they are different, then the data has changed since it was last loaded.

To do this, you need a simple way to calculate a hash. This example shows you how to calculate an MD5 hash using the .NET Framework. Other hash algorithms are also available.

Setting Up the Source and Script Component

Use the following steps to set up the source and script component:

1. Create a new package.

2. Add an OLEDB Connection Manager for your AdventureWorksDW sample database.

3. Add a Data Flow Task.

4. Add an OLEDB Source component.

5. Select the **DimAccount** table from AdventureWorksDW.

6. Add a Script Component.

7. Select it to be a Transformation component.

8. Connect the output of the OLEDB Source component to the Script Component. This Script Component will be synchronous—the script will calculate new columns for each row as it passes.

9. On the **Input Columns** tab, select **AccountType**, **AccountDescription** and **Operator**. You will calculate a single hash for these three columns. A change in any one of these columns will cause a difference in the hash calculation. Keep the **UsageType** as **ReadOnly**.

10. On the **Inputs and Outputs** tab, add one new output columns called **HashColumn**. Change its data type to **String [DT_STR]**, but you can leave its length as the default 50 characters. The hash will be 47 characters long.

Now you are ready to edit the script.

The Script

The script shown in Listing 10.2 is straightforward. Note that the script imports `System.Security.Cryptography`.

```
Imports System
Imports System.Data
Imports System.Math
Imports System.Text
Imports Microsoft.SqlServer.Dts.Pipeline.Wrapper
Imports Microsoft.SqlServer.Dts.Runtime.Wrapper
Imports System.Security.Cryptography


Public Class ScriptMain
    Inherits UserComponent
    Dim md5 As New MD5CryptoServiceProvider()
    Dim DataToHash As Byte()

    Public Overrides Sub Input0_ProcessInputRow(ByVal Row As _
        Input0Buffer)
        'Convert the string to a byte array
        DataToHash = (New UnicodeEncoding()) _
        .GetBytes( _
            Row.AccountDescription + _
            Row.AccountType + _
            Row.Operator)
```

```
        'Compute the MD5 hash algorithm
        Row.HashColumn = _
        BitConverter.ToString(md5.ComputeHash(DataToHash))
    End Sub
End Class
```

Listing 10.2: Script Component to Calculate an MD5 Hash.

Hook up the output of your script component to a RowCount component with a suitable variable for debugging. You may find it useful either to edit the source data or to try this script with another data source of your own. Figure 10.2 shows the debugging process.

FREE *Bonus:*

If you register this book at www.rationalpress.com, you can download a sample package for change data capture, which includes a text file source that you can modify for debugging.

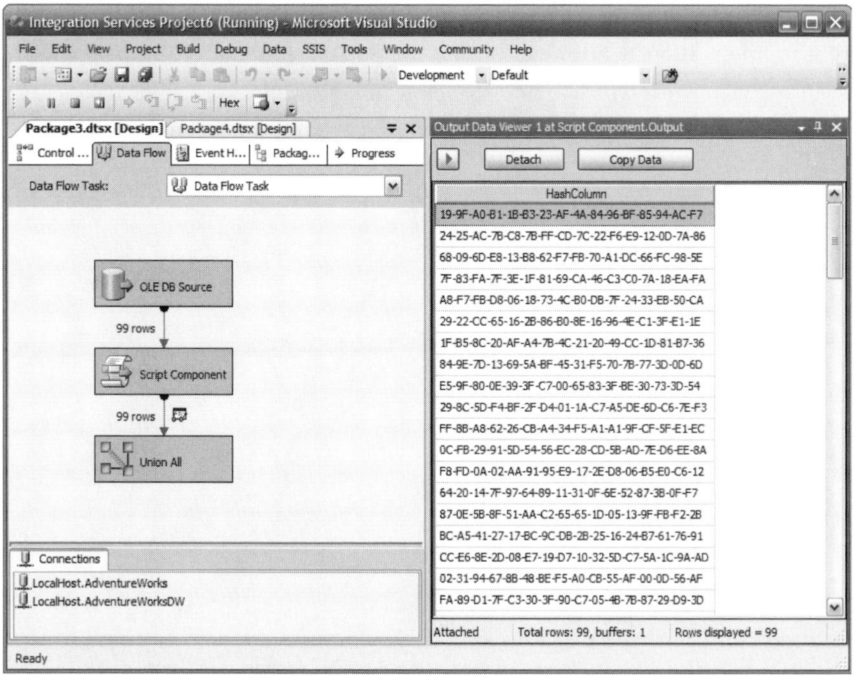

Figure 10.2: Debugging the MD5 Hash Component.

A Surrogate Key Component

Generating surrogate keys is an essential task in any data warehouse. Many users simply use Identity columns or other auto-incrementing types to generate unique keys for rows as the process inserts them. However, this does run into some issues. In particular, there are occasions when you want to know what value a surrogate key will have before inserting the row. This is often the case when loading snowflake dimensions or other parent-child table scenarios. If you are using an auto-incrementing column, then, typically, you cannot retrieve the identity until *after* inserting the row. Even then, you often cannot retrieve the identity until you have inserted an entire batch of rows and committed the transaction. This is often the case in SSIS Data Flows.

This surrogate key script solves this problem elegantly by generating keys in the Data Flow. For example, if you were splitting a row into master and detail records, you would use this script component before the split, thus ensuring that you had a new key to join those records.

The script uses a variable called *SeedValue* to store the first surrogate key value minus one. You can set the value of this seed in a number of ways. For example, you could set this value from a configuration file. However, a more common scenario would be to populate it using a SQL statement that returned the Max value of the existing keys in the table. After you have built the script, we will explain that scenario in a little more detail.

Setting Up the Source and Script Component

Use the following steps to set up the source and script component:

1. Create a new package.

2. Create a new variable named *SeedValue*.

3. Leave the data type as an integer, but change the default value to 1000.

4. Add a Data Flow Task.

5. Add an OLEDB Source Adapter.

6. Edit the source adapter. Create a connection to your AdventureWorks database.

7. Select the **[HumanResources].[Employee]** table.

8. Add a Script Component.

9. Select it to be a Transformation component.

10. Connect the output of the OLEDB Source component to the Script Component. This Script Component will be synchronous—the script will calculate new columns for each row as it passes. You do not need to select any columns on the **Input Columns** tab. Surrogate keys have no "meaning"—they are just numbers to identify a row. Therefore, they do not need to use any information from the incoming row.

11. On the **Inputs and Outputs** tab, add one new output column called **SurrogateKey**.

    Keep its data type as a four-byte integer: **[DT_I4]**.

12. On the **Script** tab, add the variable name `SeedValue` to the **ReadOnlyVariables** property.

Now you are ready to edit the script.

The Script

The script is shown in Listing 10.3 and is again very straightforward.

```
Imports System
Imports System.Data
Imports System.Math
Imports Microsoft.SqlServer.Dts.Pipeline.Wrapper
Imports Microsoft.SqlServer.Dts.Runtime.Wrapper

Public Class ScriptMain
    Inherits UserComponent
    Dim CurrentKey As Integer

    Public Overrides Sub PreExecute()
        CurrentKey = CInt(Me.Variables.SeedValue)
    End Sub
```

```
Public Overrides Sub Input0_ProcessInputRow(ByVal Row As _
    Input0Buffer)
    CurrentKey += 1
    Row.SurrogateKey = CurrentKey
End Sub
End Class
```

Listing 10.3: Surrogate Key Script Component.

Hook up the output of your script component to a RowCount component with a suitable variable for debugging. You may find it useful either to edit the source data or to try this script with some other data source of your own.

Using the Surrogate Key Script

The most common use of this script will be to generate new surrogate keys when loading a data-warehouse dimension table. In that case, you will need to find the current maximum surrogate key. The easiest way to find the current maximum key is as follows:

1. As you are loading a dimension table, we will assume that you already have created a connection manager for the database in your Package. In the Control Flow designer, drag an **Execute SQL Task** to the design surface.

2. Double-click the **Execute SQL Task** to open the **Execute SQL Task Editor**, as seen in Figure 10.3.

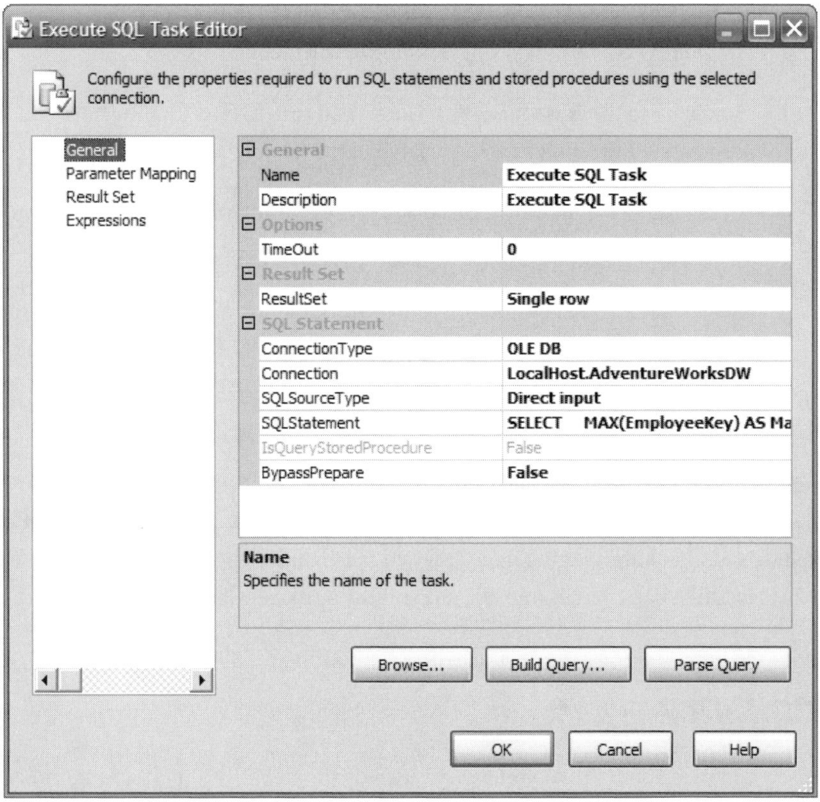

Figure 10.3: Execute SQL Task Editor.

3. On the **General** tab, for the **Connection** property, select the Connection Manager for your database.

4. The **SQLSourceType** will be **Direct Input**. You will be adding the SQL query as a property of the task.

5. In the **SQLStatement** property, enter the query to return the maximum value of the surrogate key column for your table. SSIS includes a **Query Builder**. You can click the **Build Query** button to open that dialog box. However, if you already know the SQL you wish to use, you can simply enter the code directly in the property editor. A suitable query to select a maximum surrogate key would be something like this:

```
SELECT MAX(SKey) AS MaxKey FROM MyProductDimension
```

6.   Select **SingleRow** for the **ResultSet** property. Your query will return only a single row containing a single column, **MaxKey**.

7.   Navigate to the **Result Set** tab. Click **Add** to create a mapping between the result set of the query and a variable in the package.

8.   In this case, you wish to use the **MaxKey** column in the result set. Change the value in the **Result Name** column from `NewResultName` to `MaxKey`.

9.   Select **User::SeedValue** from the drop-down list in the **Variable** column. When the task executes SSIS will store the result of the query, the value of `MaxKey`, in the *SeedValue* variable. You can now use this value in your script in the Data Flow.

Finally, add a precedence constraint between your Execute SQL Task and your Data Flow Task. In this way, the query will execute, followed by the data flow. An **OnSuccess** constraint will ensure that the data flow will not run if, for any reason, the query can not be successfully completed, and the maximum surrogate key already in use can not be determined.

Summary

These examples should give you a good idea of the flexibility of scripting in SSIS. Script is especially useful as a way of addressing business scenarios that are not quite covered by pre-built SSIS components found in the toolbox.

However, there are times when you may need to move beyond script—to create your own reusable components to add your toolbox for future projects. The next chapter introduces some of the advantages, and some of the issues you will encounter when writing SSIS custom objects.

Chapter 11

Moving Beyond Script

Script Tasks and Script Components are extremely useful for adding new functionality to your SSIS packages. They are simple to develop and test, and they deploy with the package itself. However, scripts do have some disadvantages.

Script components are very closely bound to the metadata of their specific data flow. For example, in Chapter 10, when you wrote the new surrogate key value into a column, the script used the following code:

```
Row.SurrogateKey = CurrentKey
```

As you can see, this is a very specific reference. If the column you wish to use is **SKey**, then this code will not work. You will find similar issues with connection managers and variables that you may use in the script.

It is possible to copy a Script Component or a Script Task and paste it into a new package. However, each time you do, you must also fix any direct references to columns, variables, connection managers, and so on. This may be acceptable for occasional use, but in some cases package developers will wish to reuse a substantial amount of logic, which may itself be quite complex.

For such scenarios, you can use custom code to create three types of objects that SSIS can use: assemblies, tasks, and components. These solutions have some common advantages:

▶ Assemblies are written in .NET code, so they are highly reusable—not just in SSIS, but also in other projects like Analysis Services.

▶ If written using tools hosted in Visual Studio, you can host the code projects for creating these objects in the same Visual Studio as the SSIS projects that consume them. This enables the developer to use source control across both the code and SSIS projects, ensuring they are in synchronization as versions change.

▶ You can develop these objects in any .NET language, including C#, Visual Basic .NET, J#, and other languages with .NET dialects such as COBOL, Borland Delphi and many others.

Custom Assemblies

Chapters 6, 9, and 10 showed examples of how to reference external assemblies in your script components. You may choose to wrap some functionality in a custom assembly that SSIS and other applications could call. For example, your business may use a large library of regular expressions for validating product codes, zip codes, phone numbers, customer identifiers, and so on. In this case, you could build a custom assembly containing all these expressions, exposing them as functions such as `ValidateZip`, `ValidateCustomerID` and the like.

SSIS could call these functions through a script component in the data flow to validate each row as it passes. However, as you are hosting the functions in a custom assembly, you could also call them from a front-end C# or ASP.NET application to validate user input too. This would be an effective reuse of the logic.

Useful as this solution is, the custom assemblies have no specific knowledge of SSIS. You must still handle any events, SSIS Connection Managers, or variables through the script. This still limits the reuse the between SSIS packages.

Custom Tasks and Components

In many cases, therefore, you will wish to create objects that you can easily reuse in other SSIS packages. Fortunately, even moderately skilled developers can quickly develop Control Flow Tasks and Data Flow Components for SSIS using C# or Visual Basic .NET. The SSIS documentation has many examples and code snippets that cover a wide range of scenarios: Tasks, Events, Logging, Sources, Destinations, synchronous Components, Asynchronous components, and even Connection Manager and Log Providers.

Custom tasks and components are not for your own projects only. You can share them with others too. In fact, there is a healthy ecosystem of SSIS developers and partners delivering custom tasks and components to the market.

You will find many similarities between custom tasks and components and scripts. In fact, the knowledge and skills you acquire in learning to extend SSIS with script will be of great benefit when writing custom objects.

Summary

Scripting SQL Server Integration Services is the easiest way to extend the application with new functionality. As you have seen, scripting is extremely comprehensive and gives excellent performance. In fact, scripting gives you many of the advantages of hand coding, such as precise implementation of your requirements and customization, together with the reuse of existing code and skills. However, scripting also brings the many advantages of a tool-based or application-based approach, including an application management and administration infrastructure and access to many pre-built objects.

Moving forward, you may wish to create objects that can be shared between packages or even with other users and customers. Custom tasks and components are a very effective way of doing so. However, scripting is a great foundation for learning to extend SSIS, and a good grounding in scripting techniques will give you many of the skills needed for future development with this exciting application.

Did you know?

SSIS saves your script within the package, but you can also save the script to a Visual Basic .NET file. Simply select **File→ Export** from the main menu. You can also import Visual Basic .NET files by selecting the **Project→Add Existing Item** menu item.

Glossary

.NET Framework	A Microsoft infrastructure for building and deploying Web services and other applications.
Analysis Services	The OLAP engine and services application for Microsoft SQL Server Business Intelligence. SSAS, as it is sometimes referred to, enables OLAP technologies modeled with the Unified Dimensional Model and served by a high-performance engine.
Assembly	The unit of deployment for .NET Framework code.
Asynchronous Component	In SSIS, the output of an asynchronous component is a new output and contains no rows passed from the input. The component itself must write new rows to the output explicitly. See *Synchronous*.
Buffer	An area of memory used to store rows of data as they pass through the SSIS Data Flow.
Business Intelligence (BI)	A category of related technologies for integrating, analyzing, and reporting data. Typically includes Data Warehousing.
Business Intelligence Development Studio	The version of Microsoft Visual Studio that ships with SQL Server, especially configured for developing business intelligence projects.
Class	A specific type of object used in your programming, with behaviors that you can often configure or modify. For example, a script task includes a **ScriptMain** class.
Component	In SSIS, an object which forms part of the Data Flow.

Configuration	In SSIS, a configuration is a means of saving the value of a property in an object outside the package, and then applying that property to the object when the package runs. For example, you could save the connection string of a connection to an XML file. The user could modify the connection string in the XML file. At runtime, a package configured from that XML file would read the modified connection string rather than the original value.
Connection manager	An object that manages the information needed to connect to an object such as a database or a file. Connection managers can also administer the connections from an SSIS package to those objects—for example, by enforcing restrictions on the number of connections.
Container	In SSIS, an object in the Control Flow that can contain other objects. For example, a Loop can contain Tasks. The Package itself is a container that can contain all other containers. Tasks are a special kind of container in that they have container behavior, but tasks cannot contain other tasks. See *Loop, Package, Sequence* and *Task*.
Control Flow	The workflow of an SSIS package that determines the order in which containers and tasks are executed.
Data Flow	The most important functional aspect of SSIS and the heart of the architecture. Data Flow is a group of objects, or components, which acquire data from sources, transform that data, and send it to destinations.
Data Flow Task	A specialized SSIS task that manages the objects in a Data Flow. Note: this is not an object in the Data Flow —objects *in* the Data Flow are *components*.
Data Transformation Services (DTS)	An ETL and integration utility in earlier versions of SQL Server. The predecessor to SSIS in the SQL Server Business Intelligence suite.

Data Viewer	An object that enables users to visualize data in the designer as it flows through the SSIS Data Flow.
Data Warehouse	A database whose schema is optimized for business intelligence and high performance reporting.
Destination Component	In SSIS, a component that has inputs but no regular outputs (it may have error outputs). Destinations are used typically to write data to files or databases. See *Source Component*.
Dimension	In data warehousing, a set of related entities, typically stored in a single table, or in closely related tables. For example, a data warehouse may contain Customer and Product dimension tables.
ETL	Extraction, Transformation and Loading. An application architecture for integrating business data into a data warehouse.
Event Handler	An SSIS Container that contain other containers and tasks and which executes when a given event occurs. For example, an **OnError** event handler executes a sequence of tasks when an error occurs.
Full Rowset Transformation	An asynchronous transformation, such as aggregation, that must see all the rows in a dataset before passing any rows to its output.
Input	In SSIS, a component in the Data Flow may have one or more Inputs where data arrives for processing by that component. Script components can only have one input. See *Output*.
Log Provider	An SSIS object which enables logging of package events to specific type of destination. For example, there are Log Providers that enable logging to SQL Server tables and XML files.

Loop	In SSIS, a container that iterates over objects, executing tasks within the container each time. A property of the loop enables the passing of values relating to the current object being iterated.
MD5 Hash	A number generated from a string of text. MD5 is the hash algorithm "Message Digest 5" designed by Ronald Rivest.
Namespace	A hierarchical way of arranging and managing object names, especially to make them easier to use when writing code.
Output	In SSIS, a component in the Data Flow may have one or more Outputs where data passes from that component to be processed by other components. See *Input*.
Package	An SSIS package is the container that holds all the other containers and tasks that make up a single unit of execution. That is to say, when you execute an SSIS process, you execute a package. Packages can call other packages. See *Container*.
Path	In the SSIS Data Flow, a path is the connector between two components.
Pipeline	Another name for the SSIS Data Flow.
Precedence Constraint	In the SSIS Data Flow, a Precedence Constraint is the connector between two objects such as containers or tasks. Precedence Constraints determine the conditions under which the subsequent, constrained task will execute.
Property Expression	The code written in the SSIS expression language that a task uses to set a property at runtime. For example, the Send Mail task can set its "To" property using an expression using variables such as : `@UserName + "@" + @MyDomain`.

Regular expression	A syntax that matches text strings to a pattern.
Reporting Services	The enterprise data reporting application in SQL Server Business Intelligence. See *The Rational Guide to SQL Server Reporting Services* in this series for a good general introduction.
Row Transformation	A synchronous transformation, such as Data Conversion, that can pass each row to its output as it is processed.
Rowset Transformation	An asynchronous transformation, such as Merge Join, that can create new output rows before the entire rowset has been seen. Contrast with *Full Rowset Transformation*.
Runtime	In SSIS, the Runtime Engine executes a package. An executing package is said to be in its "runtime" state, as opposed to its "design-time" state.
Scope	The section of a program where a variable can be used.
Script	A computer program embedded within your SSIS package, rather than compiled into a stand-alone object.
Sequence	In SSIS, a container whose purpose is only to contain other tasks and which has no functionality of its own.
SOUNDEX	A partially phonetic algorithm for encoding personal and other names in such a way that like-sounding values can be matched.
Source Component	In SSIS, a Data Flow component which has outputs but no regular inputs. Sources are used typically to read data from files or databases. See *Destination Component*.
SQL Server Agent	A scheduling application within SQL Server.
SQL Server Integration Services (SSIS)	The Data Integration application within the SQL Server Business Intelligence suite.

SQL Server Management Studio	The common environment for administering all SQL Server applications.
SSIS Designer	The specific environment within the Business Intelligence Development Studio for designing SSIS packages.
Subroutine	A discrete subsection of your script or a task that usually performs a specific action. For example, the PreExecute subroutine is called by SSIS just before a task executes.
Surrogate Key	A key value, usually an integer, with no semantic significance. Used only to uniquely identify members of a data warehouse dimension.
Synchronous Component	In SSIS, the output of a synchronous component does not add any rows that were not present at the input. A synchronous component can modify or add columns, but it cannot write new rows. See *Asynchronous Component*.
System Variable	A read-only named object, defined by SSIS, storing system information. For example, *UserName*, *StartTime*, etc. See *Variable*.
Task	In SSIS, a single unit of work that either succeeds or fails. For example, the Send Mail task may be set to send an e-mail, and it will either succeed or fail.
Transformation	In SSIS, a component that has both inputs and outputs. See also *Row Transformation*, *Rowset Transformation* and *Full Rowset Transformation*.
Variable	A named object of a specific type for storing a single value. See *Scope* and *System Variable*.
Visual Basic .NET	A version of Microsoft Visual Basic developed to support the Microsoft .NET Framework. The programming language used in VSA.

Visual Studio for Applications (VSA)	The development environment for writing Visual Basic .NET scripts in SSIS.

> *Note:*
>
> Terms for this glossary were extracted from the text of this book using the text mining features of SQL Server Integration Services.

Index

Learn Something New Everyday

ONLY HAVE 10 MINUTES? LEARN SOMETHING NEW AT JUMPSTARTTV.COM.

 JumpstartTV.com is a free how-to community where you can watch thousands of videos on how to do something that interest you like database technology or home improvement. There's no catches. Just great information, on-demand and when you want it. Not only can you learn from the experts but you can also be optionally be tested after you learn. Learn something new in the time it takes you to finish your coffee today.

"Just wanted to say thank you for the great videos. I've recommended that several people in our organization watch it to get them thinking. This is an amazing way to learn!"
— *Larry, Washington DC.*

Your How-To Hub ▶

Don't forget these Rational Guides to SQL Server 2005

IMPORTANT NOTICE
REGISTER YOUR BOOK

Bonus Materials

Your book refers to valuable material that complements your learning experience. In order to download these materials you will need to register your book at http://www.rationalpress.com.

This bonus material is available after registration:

► Sample code for the examples in this book

► Bonus Chapter: "Monitoring SSIS Performance with Script"

► Bonus Chapter: "Accessing Web Services with SSIS Scripts"

► Bonus Chapter: "Using SSIS as a Data Service"

Registering your book

To register your book follow these 7 easy steps:

1. Go to http://www.rationalpress.com.

2. Create an account and login.

3. Click the **My Books** link.

4. Click the **Register New Book** button.

5. Enter the registration number found on the back of the book (Figure A).

6. Confirm registration and view your new book on the virtual bookshelf.

7. Click the spine of the desired book to view the available downloads and resources for the selected book.

Figure A: Back of your book.